POP BUCHANAN

CREDIT REPAIR 2026 WITH CHATGPT

Fix Your Credit Fast with a Step-by-Step Law-Based System Using AI, Legal 609 and 611 Disputes, Trump-Era Reporting Changes, and the New 2026 Credit Rules

First published by Invest AI 2026

Research, Legal, and Accuracy Disclaimer

This book is based entirely on publicly available information from federal agencies, credit reporting companies, and verified nonprofit consumer education sources. All legal and technical explanations come from open federal documents so that readers can confirm every fact independently.

All paraphrased information is clearly identified. When a law or regulatory rule is simplified for readability, it is presented as a paraphrase of the original language. Direct quotations appear only when taken word for word from an official federal source. No invented or altered quotations appear anywhere in this book.

This material is for educational purposes only. It is not legal advice, financial advice, tax advice, or professional credit counseling. Every credit situation is different. Anyone facing a legal dispute, a collection action, an identity theft case, or a complex credit problem should speak with a licensed attorney or qualified financial professional.

Credit laws and federal interpretations change. This edition reflects the most verifiable information available for the 2025 to 2027 reporting cycle. Any links, references, or agency guidance included in this book were accurate at the time of publication. Government agencies update their websites and policies over time. Readers are encouraged to check the most recent guidance on official government websites such as the Consumer Financial Protection Bureau and the Federal Trade Commission.

This book will be updated annually. Credit reporting rules, consumer protection policies, and scoring models evolve. Future editions will be released to reflect any material changes in law or federal interpretation that affect consumers.

Neither the author nor any affiliated companies guarantee results. You are responsible for any actions you take using the information in this book. Pop Buchanan, Invest AI, Sober Is Dope, and all related companies, imprints, or brands are not liable for any financial loss, legal outcome, dispute result, or consequence arising from the use of this content.

All references to ChatGPT are for educational and research purposes only. ChatGPT does not provide legal advice. ChatGPT does not make credit decisions. ChatGPT does not contact credit bureaus or creditors on your behalf. ChatGPT helps you understand information, organize your documents, and draft letters in plain language. You remain responsible for all actions you take with your credit reports and all communications you send.

OpenAI is not affiliated with this book. OpenAI did not sponsor, endorse, review, or participate in the creation of this book. All uses of ChatGPT in the credit repair process are voluntary, educational, and user directed. ChatGPT is a tool, not a legal representative or credit repair service.

Every effort has been made to ensure accuracy and integrity. If a claim could not be verified through open public sources, it was not included. Errors of interpretation or updates in federal policy after publication are unintentional. Readers should always cross-check major financial decisions with the most current information available.

This book exists for one purpose. To help you understand your rights, protect yourself, and rebuild your credit with clarity, accuracy, confidence, and lawful steps.

First edition

This book was professionally typeset on Reedsy.
Find out more at reedsy.com

Contents

Introduction

The New Credit World and What You Will Learn in This Book

Credit in America has never been more confusing than it is today. Rules are shifting. Court decisions collide with state laws. Medical debt rules change one month and freeze the next. Student loan protections ended. SBA loans resurfaced. People hear rumors about bureaus being replaced, medical debt being erased, 609 letters fixing everything overnight, and Trump era reversals happening in real time. The internet makes everything sound urgent, political, or impossible. The truth is far simpler. This book exists to give you the truth in plain, steady language without fear, hype, or confusion.

This book is for the person who feels overwhelmed. For the person who opens their credit report and feels lost. For the person who cannot hire a credit repair company or attorney. For the person who has been misled by shortcuts, bad advice, and old myths. For the person who believes seven years is their only option. For the person who needs a real, proven, legal, and calm system to rebuild credit with dignity.

Credit determines where you live, what you drive, how much you pay, and how safe you feel when life shifts. When your credit is strong, you feel grounded. When it is damaged, you feel trapped. Many people believe their score defines their worth. It does not. Credit is data. Credit is paperwork. Credit can be fixed. You simply need real information and clear steps.

In this book, you will learn everything the credit bureaus never explain. You will learn how the three major bureaus work, how they verify information, and how federal law gives you the right to correct what is wrong. You will learn the rules that protect you, including the Fair Credit Reporting Act, the Fair Debt Collection Practices Act, and the rights that lenders must follow whether they like it or not.

You will learn how to pull your real credit reports from the official source. You will learn how to read every line. You will learn how to find what is accurate, what is wrong, and what is harming your score. You will learn exactly what a good credit score means in 2026, why the definition is changing, and what lenders expect during a rebuild.

You will learn the truth behind the headlines. You will learn how medical debt reporting changed after the Trump era announcements and how federal preemption overrides state bans. You will learn what actually changed during the Biden years, especially with student loans and collections. You will learn why SBA EIDL and PPP loans sometimes show up on reports and sometimes do not. You will learn what the IRS can report and why most of it never touches your credit file. You will learn the real rules behind EBT, SNAP, and government benefits so you never fear misinformation again.

You will learn the deep structure of your score. You will learn how utilization works. You will learn how late payments damage your file. You will learn how paying before the reporting date boosts your score. You will learn how specialty consumer reporting agencies like LexisNexis, SageStream, CoreLogic, Innovis, ChexSystems, and others influence everything from disputes to identity verification. You will learn how freezing or unfreezing these agencies affects the outcome of a reinvestigation.

You will learn the full truth about disputes. You will learn what to dispute, what not to dispute, and what happens inside the bureaus when they reinvestigate. You will learn why online disputes weaken your rights. You will learn how to create a paper trail. You will learn the difference between

Section 609 and Section 611. You will learn why 609 is a popular myth and why 611 is the legal backbone that gets results. You will learn how to avoid re aging, how to handle zombie debt, how to negotiate settlements, and how pay for delete agreements work when done ethically and legally.

You will learn how to rebuild with new positive history. You will learn how to use secured cards the right way. You will learn how builder loans work. You will learn how rent reporting and utility reporting strengthen your profile, and you will learn the top companies that offer these services. You will learn the truth about authorized users and when to avoid them. You will learn how tradelines work in the real world. You will learn how Buy Now Pay Later companies like Klarna, Afterpay, Affirm, PayPal Pay in 4, Chime MyPay, and Empower Loans affect your credit in 2026. You will learn how an auto loan can build your credit or damage it and how to avoid the dealer hard inquiry shotgun trap that ruins thousands of scores every year.

You will learn how to protect yourself from fraud. You will learn how to freeze your credit. You will learn how fraud alerts work. You will learn how to handle identity theft. You will learn when federal law requires guaranteed deletions. You will learn how statute of limitations rules affect collection rights and why a debt can stop being collectible but still appear on your report for seven years. You will learn how to avoid restarting old debt with one mistake.

You will learn how to use the CFPB complaint system. You will learn how to escalate errors when furnishers or bureaus fail to follow the law. You will learn how to document everything. You will learn how to protect yourself from credit repair scams and how to recognize false promises that violate federal law.

You will learn how to build business credit. You will learn how personal credit supports business credit. You will learn how to open the right accounts. You will learn how to structure your first steps without falling into predatory traps.

You will learn the full ninety day reset plan and the six month rebuild plan. You will learn how to prepare for home ownership. You will learn when bankruptcy is necessary and when it is not. You will learn how to rebuild your emotional confidence along with your financial life.

And you will learn how to use ChatGPT as a real assistant. You will learn how AI helps you read your reports, write clear letters, stay organized, compare accounts, understand legal language, draft responses, and build your timelines. You will learn what AI can do and what it cannot do. You will learn how to ask questions safely and how to use ChatGPT as a partner every step of the way.

This book also gives you a real case study of a man who lost everything during the pandemic and rebuilt himself from the ground up. His path gives you a living example of what is possible. And behind every chapter sits my own journey, my fall, my recovery, my rebuild, and the steady habits that lifted my score and my life.

This book is not only a guide. It is a system. It is a companion. It is a map. It gives you every tool the average person was never taught. It replaces fear with clarity. It replaces shame with structure. It replaces confusion with calm steps.

Credit repair is not magic. It is law. It is sequence. It is discipline. It is knowledge. And now you have all of it.

1

How to Use ChatGPT to Repair Your Credit Safely and Effectively

This chapter appears first for a reason. You bought this book, in part, because you want to know if ChatGPT or any AI tool can help you fix your credit in a safe and simple way. You may feel overwhelmed by credit reports. You may wonder how to write dispute letters. You may be unsure which steps to take first. AI can help you understand everything in this book. It can help you organize, plan, and move through the credit repair process at a steady pace. It cannot replace an attorney or a financial professional, but it can help you think clearly and act with structure. That is why this chapter comes before we dive into the laws, the reporting system, the Trump and Biden updates, and the step by step credit rebuilding process.

AI does not make decisions for you. You stay in control. AI helps you read information, outline letters, summarize reports, create schedules, and prepare for each chapter that follows. Think of ChatGPT as a tool that turns confusion into order. It helps you understand what you see on your reports. It helps you explain your thoughts on paper. It helps you remove emotion when writing letters. It helps you prepare for calls with creditors. And it helps you plan the rebuild process one step at a time.

The first way to use ChatGPT is to help you read your credit reports. Many people feel lost when they open their files. Reports are filled with long account numbers, dates, balances, and codes that repeat across three different bureaus. If you copy the text of an account into ChatGPT, the AI can help you explain it in simple language. You do not need to give your Social Security number or full account numbers. You can remove sensitive details. The AI can still help you understand the structure of the report. It can help you see whether dates line up. It can help you list high balances, missed payments, or mistakes. It cannot tell you if an item is valid or not, but it can help you read it.

The second way AI helps is by comparing your reports. Different bureaus sometimes show different information. You can paste data from each report and ask ChatGPT to list the differences. The AI can show you if one bureau shows a late payment while another shows a clean history. The AI can point out if a balance is missing from one file or if a paid collection is still showing as unpaid somewhere else. You will be surprised by how many differences appear once the AI organizes the information.

Another important use for ChatGPT is drafting letters. A dispute letter must be calm, factual, and based on clear information. Many people add emotion to their letters because credit problems are stressful. When a letter includes emotion or long explanations, it may confuse the process. AI helps you stay focused. You can tell ChatGPT the issue and ask it to write a simple factual letter. You can ask it to remove personal feelings and keep only the core facts. You must still check the letter. You must still attach your documents. But the AI helps you build the letter with clear language.

ChatGPT can also help you keep track of time. The credit bureaus have limited time to investigate disputes. You can tell the AI when you mailed your letter, and it can help you create a timeline for the next steps. It can also help you list your letters, your documents, your certified mail receipts, and your responses. This helps you stay organized, especially if you are disputing many accounts at once.

Another way AI helps is by preparing scripts for phone calls. If you need to speak with a creditor or a collector, you can ask ChatGPT to help you write a script. You can tell the AI what you want to say, and it can help you shape your words in a calm and simple tone. This helps you avoid saying things that may harm your credit or restart old debts. It helps you talk with confidence.

ChatGPT can also help you plan your rebuild. You can ask it to help you choose which positive accounts to add. You can ask it to help you budget your payments. You can ask it to help you create a plan for the next three to six months. AI has a talent for taking many ideas and organizing them into a clean list.

This book was written with the help of AI. This is why this chapter sits at the front. It teaches you how to use the book with the same tool that helped create it. It also helps you get better at communicating your thoughts. If you want a full guide on writing better prompts for any use, you can read my other book titled ChatGPT Writing Secrets. It teaches you how to talk to AI with clarity so you get the results you want.

Here is how to use ChatGPT with this book:

- You begin with this chapter.
- You pull your reports when you finish reading it.
- You feed parts of your reports into ChatGPT to help you understand them.
- You move to the chapters on your rights and the dispute process.
- You ask ChatGPT to help you outline your letters.
- You follow the steps in the book chapter by chapter.
- You keep ChatGPT as your partner through the whole journey.

This chapter exists to give you all the tools you need before you begin the work. It is the key that unlocks the rest of the book. It reduces fear. It reduces confusion. It makes the process smoother.

The safest way to use AI is simple. Do not share sensitive details. You can remove account numbers and personal information. You can keep the focus on the part of the report that you want to understand. You stay in control of every detail.

Below is a full set of prompts you can use at different stages of the credit repair process. All of these prompts keep you safe and help you use the book effectively.

Prompt to read your report:

"Here is the text from a section of my credit report. Can you help me explain what these dates and balances mean in simple language?"

Prompt to compare different bureaus:

"Here are two versions of the same account from different bureaus. Can you help me list the differences?"

Prompt to spot possible errors:

"Can you help me identify details that look inconsistent in this section of my credit report based only on the text I provide?"

Prompt to draft a dispute letter:

"I believe this account is incorrect. Here are the details. Can you help me draft a simple factual letter without legal advice?"

Prompt to remove emotion from a letter:

"Here is a letter I wrote. Can you help me rewrite it in calm and factual language?"

Prompt to organize your dispute timeline:
"I mailed a dispute letter on this date. Can you help me build a timeline for what happens next?"

Prompt to build a positive credit plan:
"I want to rebuild my credit. Can you help me make a simple plan for the next three months based on these goals?"

Prompt to prepare a phone script:
"I need to call a collector about this account. Can you help me write a calm and clear script?"

Prompt to create a money plan:
"Can you help me build a simple budget for the next two months based on these expenses?"

These prompts turn AI into a credit repair partner. You still make the choices. You still sign the letters. You still send the mail. AI helps you stay steady and clear.

This chapter is here because AI changes the way you handle credit repair. It makes the process less heavy. It gives you clarity when you feel lost. It gives you structure when your thoughts feel scattered. It gives you a way to move forward without fear.

Now that you know how to use ChatGPT with this book, you can move into the next chapters with confidence. You will learn the laws that protect you. You will learn how reports work. You will learn how to dispute. You will learn how to rebuild. AI will stay with you from start to finish. This is how the credit repair journey becomes simple and possible.

2

The Credit System Is Built Against You, but You Can Win

Credit in America is like a file that follows you wherever you go. It records how you borrow, how you pay, and where you fall behind. That file does not know your story. It does not see your recovery, your bad year, your layoff, or your grief. It only responds to numbers and patterns. The system was not designed to understand people. It was designed to measure risk for lenders.

At the center of this system are three large private companies. They are Equifax, Experian, and TransUnion. These companies are called credit reporting agencies or credit bureaus. They collect information about your credit accounts, your payment history, your balances, your credit limits, some public records, and some collection accounts, then they sell that information to lenders and others who are allowed by law to see it. Together they are known as the three nationwide consumer reporting agencies. (paraphrase based on Consumer Financial Protection Bureau, 2021; Equifax Inc., 2024)

The main federal law that governs these files is the Fair Credit Reporting Act, often called the FCRA. The FCRA is meant to promote accuracy, fairness, and privacy in the files kept by consumer reporting agencies. It gives you the right to see what is in your file, to get a free report at regular intervals, and to dispute information you believe is wrong or incomplete. It also requires the bureaus and the companies that furnish information to them to investigate disputes and to correct or delete data that cannot be verified. (paraphrase based on Federal Trade Commission, 2016)

Most people do not see any of this. They only see a score. A credit score is a three digit number that comes from the information in your reports. FICO is the most widely used scoring brand. FICO has explained that its scores are built from five main categories of information. These are your payment history, the amounts you owe, the length of your credit history, your new credit activity, and your mix of different types of credit. Payment history is the largest part, followed by how much you owe. The other three categories have smaller weights but still matter. (paraphrase based on Consumer Financial Protection Bureau, 2020; myFICO, 2024)

This is why scores feel harsh. One late payment can hurt a file that was clean for years. When balances rise close to your limits, your score can fall even if you have never missed a payment. When you open several new accounts in a short period, your score can dip again. FICO and other education sources explain that these changes are normal and that the system is reacting to markers of risk. (paraphrase based on Consumer Financial Protection Bureau, 2020; National Foundation for Credit Counseling, 2024)

The system feels rigged for another reason. The bureaus collect huge amounts of information from banks, card companies, debt collectors, and other furnishers, but they do not check every detail before it lands in your file. The law does not require them to prove each item in advance. Instead, the FCRA gives you the right to challenge items you believe are wrong. Once you dispute something, the bureau must reinvestigate. It must ask the furnisher to confirm the information. If the furnisher cannot confirm it, the bureau must correct or delete it within set timelines. (paraphrase based on Federal Trade Commission, 2016)

Most people never use this right. They may never look at their full reports. They may assume that a low score means they are simply bad with money. In reality, many reports contain errors. Common problems include accounts that do not belong to you, old addresses that tie your file to another person, wrong dates for late payments, debts that are reported more than once, or collection accounts that should show as paid but still look open. Some errors come from identity theft. Others come from simple data mix ups. Because the system is automated, small errors can spread and stay in place for years if no one challenges them. (paraphrase based on Consumer Financial Protection Bureau, 2021)

You are not powerless here. Federal law gives you the right to see each of your three reports at no charge on a regular basis. The only website that is authorized by law to provide your free nationwide reports is AnnualCreditReport dot com. The Federal Trade Commission has warned that other sites may charge fees or pretend to be the official site in order to capture your data. At AnnualCreditReport dot com you can request your Equifax, Experian, and TransUnion reports and review them for errors. (paraphrase based on Federal Trade Commission, 2024)

These reports will not always match each other. Some lenders report to all three bureaus. Some report to only one or two. That is why you can have three different scores at the same time. A lender might see your best file or your worst file depending on which bureau it uses. This is another way the system feels tilted. Even when you are careful, the picture that a lender sees may not be complete.

There is another layer that most people do not see at all. Behind the three main bureaus are specialty and secondary consumer reporting agencies. Some track check writing history. Some track rental history. Some track medical or insurance data. Others are large data brokers that help verify information for the big three. They are part of the larger credit reporting network and they are also covered by the FCRA. You will meet these agencies in later chapters, where we show how freezing certain files can affect disputes and verifications. (paraphrase based on Federal Trade Commission, 2016; Consumer Financial Protection Bureau, 2024)

For now, the key idea is simple. The credit system is not neutral. It favors lenders. It moves quickly when you make a mistake and slowly when you try to fix one. It will not fix itself on your behalf. But it is also not random. It is built on laws, on data, and on rules that are written down. Once you understand those rules, you can start to use them for yourself instead of feeling crushed by them.

This book exists to give you that map. The next chapter explains your legal rights under the main federal laws that protect you, including the FCRA, the Fair Debt Collection Practices Act, the Equal Credit Opportunity Act, and the Credit Repair Organizations Act. Later chapters walk through how to pull and read your real reports, how to use factual disputes, how to deal with medical debt, student loans, SBA loans, and tax issues in the current policy climate, and how to work with specialty consumer reporting agencies. Then we shift into building and rebuilding. You will learn how to add positive accounts, how to manage utilization, how to negotiate with collectors, how to avoid scams, and how to build toward home ownership and business credit.

You do not need to master everything at once. You only need to learn enough to take the next step. The credit system is built against the average person, but it is also mechanical. When you learn how it works, you can begin to repair it. Your past mistakes, your hardest years, and the chaos of your old life do not have to decide your future score. Your reports can change. Your score can move. With time, simple habits, and clear use of your rights, you can move from confusion and shame to structure and control. This book will guide you through that process, one chapter at a time.

3

Your Legal Rights Nobody Explains

Most people try to repair their credit without learning the laws that shape the system. They try advice from friends, social media, or paid companies, and most of that advice has nothing to do with what the law actually says. Credit feels confusing because the rules sit inside several federal laws, and those laws are written for lawyers instead of regular people. When you understand these laws, credit repair stops feeling random. It becomes a simple process based on rights that belong to you. This chapter explains those rights in clear language so you know the power you already have.

The first and most important law is the Fair Credit Reporting Act. This law gives you the right to see your credit reports and the right to dispute information that is wrong or incomplete. The Federal Trade Commission explains that the law is meant to support accuracy, fairness, and privacy in credit files. (paraphrase based on Federal Trade Commission, 2016) The law requires the credit bureaus to investigate your dispute. It also requires the company that supplied the information to check its own records. If the company cannot prove the information is correct, the bureau must delete it or fix it. This is the legal base for every real dispute. The law does not require the bureaus to check every item before it goes into your file, but once you challenge something, they must take action.

The next law is the Fair Debt Collection Practices Act. This law does not change your credit report by itself. Instead, it protects you when collectors contact you. The Consumer Financial Protection Bureau explains that the Act prohibits harassment, false statements, and unfair conduct from debt collectors. (paraphrase based on Consumer Financial Protection Bureau, 2020) During credit repair, you may receive calls or letters from collectors. You need to know what they can and cannot do. A collector cannot threaten jail. A collector cannot lie about the amount you owe. A collector cannot claim they will take legal action if they cannot do so. If the debt is not yours, you have the right to dispute it, and they must respond honestly.

Another major protection is the Equal Credit Opportunity Act. This law focuses on fair access to credit. It says a creditor cannot treat you differently because of your race, color, religion, national origin, sex, marital status, age, or because you receive public assistance. The CFPB explains that creditors must evaluate applications based on credit factors, not who the applicant is. (paraphrase based on Consumer Financial Protection Bureau, 2024) This matters when you start applying for new accounts. Your credit score may limit your choices, but discrimination is illegal. If you are denied for reasons that violate this law, you have the right to take action.

The last major law tied to credit repair is the Credit Repair Organizations Act. This law exists because many companies made false promises in the past. They charged people high fees and claimed they could erase accurate negative information. CROA makes it illegal for a credit repair company to lie about what it can do. The Federal Trade Commission explains that CROA forbids companies from promising to delete accurate negative items and forbids them from charging before services are done. (paraphrase based on Federal Trade Commission, 2016) The law does not stop companies from offering help, but it blocks the most harmful practices. It also requires them to give you a written contract that explains your rights.

When you understand these laws, the whole process becomes clearer. The credit bureaus must investigate your disputes. The companies that report information must check their records. Debt collectors must follow strict rules when they contact you. Creditors must treat you fairly when you apply for new accounts. Credit repair companies cannot make claims that violate federal law. These are not favors. These are rights.

Credit repair becomes easier once you see this structure. You are not begging a bureau to show mercy. You are using the rights already given to you by federal law. Accuracy is required. Verification is required. Fair treatment is required. These laws give you a solid base to challenge errors and rebuild your credit with confidence.

4

Credit Repair Scams

Credit repair is one of the most misunderstood industries because many people feel desperate when their score drops. Scammers know this. They target people who feel stressed, afraid, or ashamed. They promise miracles, overnight deletions, and secret legal loopholes that do not exist. This chapter protects you from the traps that have hurt thousands of people.

A real credit repair service will never promise to delete accurate negative information. No company can erase late payments you actually made. No company can guarantee removal of bankruptcies, repossessions, or charge offs that are reported accurately. Any company making those promises is breaking the law.

A real credit repair service will never ask you to lie. They will not tell you to claim that accounts are fraudulent when they are not. They will not tell you to dispute every account on your file. They will not tell you to build a new identity or apply for a "credit profile number," which is illegal. They will follow the Fair Credit Reporting Act and use your real rights without fabricating information.

A real company will never charge you before performing work. The Credit Repair Organizations Act forbids advance fees. You must receive a written contract, a clear description of the services, and a notice of cancellation rights. If a company pressures you to pay upfront, walks you through a rushed process, or refuses to explain the law, you walk away.

One of the biggest scams in recent years is the rise of template letter companies that promise mass deletions. These letters often carry the same wording across thousands of consumers. The bureaus detect this immediately and flag them as frivolous. Another modern scam involves "AI delete everything tools" that claim to wipe your report clean. AI can help you analyze your report and draft letters, but it cannot break the law or force deletions.

Scammers also target people with government benefits. They claim they can remove EBT issues, remove medical debt, remove student loans, or remove taxes automatically. They cannot. They target people who are stressed about the economy and promise relief. You protect yourself by understanding the reporting rules and by knowing that real credit repair is slow, steady, and built on accuracy.

This book teaches you the same methods that legitimate, law-abiding credit repair professionals use. Knowledge protects you. Scams disappear when you step into the process with clarity. Credit repair is powerful, but only when it is done honestly and legally.

5

Pulling and Reading Your Real Credit Reports

Most people try to fix their credit without ever looking at the document that shapes their financial life. They rely on scores from apps, quick summaries, or alerts that show only the surface. None of that gives you the full picture. The only way to repair your credit the right way is to pull your complete reports from all three bureaus and read them line by line. This chapter explains how to get the correct reports, why they matter, and how to interpret them without confusion.

Federal law gives you the right to access your credit reports for free once every twelve months from each bureau. The Consumer Financial Protection Bureau explains that you are entitled to these reports under the Fair Credit Reporting Act and that the official place to request them is AnnualCreditReport dot com (CFPB, 2024). This site is authorized by federal law and remains the single legitimate source where the three bureaus must provide your full files. Downloading anything from anywhere else will not give you the legal versions you need for dispute work.

The reports from Equifax, Experian and TransUnion will not look the same. This is normal. Lenders choose which bureaus they report to, so one bureau may show accounts that the others do not. A collection might appear on one report and not the others. An old address might show up in one file and be missing in the next. These differences do not mean something is wrong. They simply show how fragmented the reporting system is. The Federal Trade Commission states that not all furnishers report to every bureau, which is why the files may differ (FTC, 2023). This is the reason credit repair must be done on all three reports, not just one.

Reading the reports takes patience. They are not written for regular people. They are written for automated systems and financial institutions. The first step is to slow down and read each item without assuming it makes sense. Most negative items are easy to spot because they stand out. Collections show up with the name of the collector, the original creditor, the balance and the date reported. Late payments show up as thirty, sixty or ninety day marks on a trade line. Public records, such as bankruptcies, appear in their own section if they exist. Your job is to observe, not to judge. This part is about gathering information before you challenge anything.

The most important part of reading your reports is identifying what does not belong. An error can be as simple as a wrong date. It can be a balance that is no longer correct. Sometimes it is a duplicate account that appears twice after being sold from one collector to another. Sometimes it is an account that is not yours at all. The Federal Trade Commission warns that errors can include mixed files, outdated information, incorrect payment history and inaccurate account status, all of which can hurt your score (FTC, 2024). These errors are what you will dispute later. For now, the goal is to highlight them so you know what needs attention.

You will also see items that hurt to look at but are accurate. Missed payments, old overdrawn accounts and collections that belong to you may still be painful to see, but the law does not allow you to dispute them simply because they are negative. Disputes work only when the information is inaccurate or cannot be verified. That rule comes directly from the Fair Credit Reporting Act, which requires bureaus to remove or correct information that is inaccurate, incomplete or unverifiable, but allows them to report accurate negative information for up to seven years (FTC, 2023). Understanding that difference saves you from wasting time and energy on disputes that will not succeed.

One of the common myths about credit reports is the idea of a soft delete. People sometimes believe that if a negative item drops off one report temporarily, it means the repair is complete. In reality, the disappearance of an item often means nothing more than a delay in posting or a change in the furnisher's reporting schedule. A true deletion means the item is removed after an investigation or because the reporting period has expired. A temporary disappearance is not proof of correction. Only the dispute process or the passage of time triggers real deletions.

As you read your reports, keep notes on every item that looks wrong, unclear or questionable. You will need these notes in later chapters when you begin the dispute process. Reading your reports with accuracy is the foundation for everything that follows. It is the moment when you see your financial story laid out without judgment, without explanations and without context. It is also the moment when you gain control. When you learn how to read these documents, the system stops feeling mysterious. You know what is being reported about you, and you know why your score looks the way it does. That knowledge is the first step toward rebuilding your credit and your sense of financial strength.

6

The Verified Dispute Method That Really Works

The dispute process is the core of legitimate credit repair. It is not a loophole or a trick. It is a federal right that forces the credit bureaus and the companies that report information about you to prove that their records are accurate. When you know how to use this right correctly, you stop feeling powerless inside a system that often works against you. You begin using the law the way it was written, and the law is clear about your ability to challenge errors in your file.

The Fair Credit Reporting Act creates the rules for disputes. The Federal Trade Commission explains that the credit reporting agencies must investigate items that you challenge unless your dispute does not contain enough information to evaluate it (paraphrase based on FTC, 2023). This requirement is the foundation of the entire process. A bureau cannot ignore you when you tell them something is wrong. They must begin a reinvestigation and contact the company that furnished the information.

Once the bureau receives your dispute, they must share it with the furnisher. The Federal Trade Commission notes that the furnisher must review the information sent by the bureau and check its own records to determine whether the entry is accurate (paraphrase based on FTC, 2023). This is the moment when the burden shifts away from you. You no longer need to prove anything. The furnisher must confirm the accuracy of what they reported. If they cannot confirm it with evidence, the law requires the bureau to correct or delete the item.

People weaken their rights when they file disputes online through credit monitoring apps or bureau portals. These portals are designed for convenience, not protection. Online systems may limit the types of documents you can upload or may not preserve detailed records of your submissions. Attorneys avoid them because they do not provide the same evidentiary trail that mailed disputes provide. When you mail a dispute, you create a permanent record of what you sent, when you sent it and what evidence accompanied it. That record protects you if a bureau later claims it did not receive something.

A true dispute is simple and factual. You identify the item. You explain the inaccuracy. You provide documentation if you have it. You do not need to tell a story or explain hardship. You are not requesting sympathy. You are asserting your right to accurate reporting. When you do this with clarity, the system must respond. The law does not give the bureaus freedom to delay or ignore disputes without reason. They must act within the timelines set by federal law, which generally require resolution within thirty days unless specific extensions apply.

Sometimes a bureau may tell you that your dispute is frivolous. The Consumer Financial Protection Bureau states that if a bureau labels a dispute frivolous, it must notify you and explain what additional information it needs to continue the investigation (paraphrase based on CFPB, 2024). This notice is not a rejection. It is a request for more details. When you supply the missing information, the bureau must proceed.

The key rule that governs every dispute is simple. The credit bureaus must remove information that is inaccurate, incomplete or cannot be verified. This is part of the structure of the Fair Credit Reporting Act. The law does not require them to delete accurate negative information simply because you do not like it. It requires them to ensure that everything in your file is correct. When a furnisher fails to verify an entry, the system must correct it. This is why factual disputes work. They rely on accuracy, not persuasion.

When you dispute an item correctly, you are using the law as it was intended. You are holding the bureaus and furnishers accountable for the information they publish about you. The process may take time, but it is reliable because it is built into federal regulation. Once you learn how to use it, you stop guessing. You know exactly what the law requires, and you follow the steps that lead to results.

7

Credit Repair Under President Trump and President Biden, Myths and Reality

Credit repair videos online make it sound like presidents can erase negative items with a signature. They say Trump "killed the credit bureaus," or Biden "made late payments illegal," or "new laws force deletions." None of these claims match the public record. The truth is simpler, based on published federal actions, court rulings, and real guidance from the agencies that run the credit system.

The most important credit change linked to Trump's first term happened in 2018 when he signed the Economic Growth, Regulatory Relief, and Consumer Protection Act. This law made credit freezes free nationwide and extended initial fraud alerts from ninety days to one year (Federal Trade Commission, 2018). Before this law, many people paid to freeze or unfreeze their files. Afterward, anyone could freeze Equifax, Experian, and TransUnion without cost.

During the same period, the Trump administration opposed the Protecting Your Credit Score Act of 2019, a bill that would have created a federal portal combining all three credit reports and scores. The administration publicly opposed the bill in a Statement of Administration Policy (White House, 2019).

The bill never became law, showing that there was no federal effort to replace or eliminate the three credit bureaus.

Under Biden, most changes were tied to emergency protections during the pandemic. The CARES Act paused payments and negative reporting for most federal student loans. These protections expired when repayment resumed in 2023. Biden also supported the Fresh Start program, which temporarily kept defaulted federal student loans from reporting as negative. Fresh Start ended in 2024. These programs helped borrowers during a crisis but did not permanently change how student loans report.

Biden's administration also pushed for major changes to medical debt. In 2022, the CFPB announced that small medical collections under five hundred dollars would no longer appear on credit reports. The three bureaus then voluntarily removed many medical collections (Consumer Financial Protection Bureau, 2022). In early 2025, the CFPB issued a rule that would have banned medical bills from credit reports and barred lenders from using medical debt in credit decisions. That rule never took effect. In July 2025, a federal judge in Texas vacated the rule (public reporting, 2025). The CFPB did not appeal.

Soon after Trump returned to office, the CFPB issued an interpretive rule stating that the Fair Credit Reporting Act overrides certain state laws that ban medical debt reporting (public reporting, 2025). This means federal law controls the reporting rules and state bans cannot erase medical debt from national credit files.

These actions are the only confirmed policy changes. No administration passed a law that erases accurate late payments. No administration required bureaus to delete collections. No administration eliminated credit bureaus. The core laws that matter for credit repair remain the Fair Credit Reporting Act, the Fair Debt Collection Practices Act, the Equal Credit Opportunity Act, and the Credit Repair Organizations Act. These laws determine dispute rights, reporting limits, collector behavior, and what credit repair companies are allowed to promise.

Online rumors grow because people want shortcuts. They want one letter or one law to clean their file. But the credit system is grounded in long standing federal law. Presidents influence parts of the system, but they cannot override the legal structure that governs accuracy, verification, dispute timelines, and reporting rules.

There are real benefits you can use under Trump's current administration. Free freezes give you control over your reports. Longer fraud alerts create more identity protection. A single national standard for medical debt reporting makes the rules clearer across states. And the unchanged dispute rights under the FCRA continue to give you the power to correct errors, challenge outdated information, and rebuild your file with accuracy.

These tools may not sound dramatic, but they are consistent and real. They give you control, clarity, and protection. They allow you to rebuild the same way every skilled credit repair attorney does. With steady steps, you can still raise your score, remove mistakes, and rebuild a financial life based on truth.

Credit repair does not depend on political rumors. It depends on using your rights. When you follow the actual law, you are not chasing trends. You are using a system that was built to correct itself when you speak up.

8

How Student Loans Affect Your Credit in 2026

Student loans have changed many times over the last few years. These changes can make people feel confused or lost. In 2026 the rules are more stable, but they are different from what many people remember during the COVID years. This chapter explains what can be confirmed from public information and helps you understand how student loans now show up on credit reports.

During the COVID emergency, the federal government paused payments and stopped interest on many federal student loans. For a long time, late payments and missed payments on these loans did not hurt credit scores because the loans were not being reported as past due. This protection ended. The payment pause is no longer in place. People with federal student loans must make payments again. If payments are missed, those missed payments can now appear on credit reports.

There was also a temporary program called Fresh Start. This program helped people who were in default on their federal student loans. It let many borrowers move out of default and gave them a chance to repair their credit. Fresh Start also prevented negative reporting during the program.

This program ended. Now the normal rules apply again for defaulted federal student loans.

When payments are due and not made, student loan servicers may report those missed payments to credit bureaus. This is allowed under the Fair Credit Reporting Act, as long as the information is accurate and complete. A missed payment can hurt a credit score, and several missed payments can hurt even more. Defaulted loans may also lead to collection actions, which can appear on credit reports if the information is correct.

Even though these protections ended, you still have rights. If you think your student loan account has been reported the wrong way, you can dispute the information. For example, if you were in a special plan or a temporary hold and the servicer still reported you as late, you can ask for the record to be corrected. You can contact your servicer and ask for a record of your payment history. You can compare their records to yours. If something looks wrong, you can send a dispute to the credit bureau. The bureau must investigate. If the servicer cannot verify the information, the bureau must fix it.

If you are struggling with payments, the safest step is to contact your servicer right away. Federal student loans have several repayment plans. Income driven repayment plans can lower your monthly payment based on your income and family size. These plans can help prevent missed payments and protect your credit. Servicers must explain these plans when you ask. You can apply online or by phone. When the payment is affordable, it is easier to stay on track and avoid negative marks.

If your loan is in default, you still have options. You can ask about loan rehabilitation. This is a process that helps you make a set number of on time monthly payments. When you complete rehabilitation, the default can be removed from your credit report. You can also look at consolidation. This can sometimes take a loan out of default and give you a fresh start with a new repayment plan. These steps take time, but they can protect your future.

Private student loans follow different rules. Private lenders set their own terms, but they still must report accurate information. If a private loan is reported wrong, you can dispute it the same way you dispute any other account. You can ask the lender for records. You can ask the credit bureau to investigate. If the lender cannot prove the information, the bureau must correct it.

Student loans can feel heavy and confusing. Many people carry them for years. Even so, you have tools that help you stay safe. You can check your reports. You can correct errors. You can request payment plans that fit your life. You can work your way out of default. Your credit can improve when you stay steady and use your rights.

This chapter gives you the facts that are true today. Student loans are now reported again. Missed payments can hurt your score. Federal protections from the COVID period are no longer active. But your rights under the Fair Credit Reporting Act remain strong. When you use them, you can protect your credit and stay in control of your future.

9

How Medical Debt Works on Credit Reports in 2026

Medical debt is confusing because the rules feel like they change often. Some bills are removed from credit reports, and some can still show up. This chapter explains only what can be confirmed from public sources. Nothing here comes from guesswork. This is the safest and clearest way to understand medical debt and your credit in 2026.

The three major credit bureaus made public changes to how they handle medical collection debt in 2022 and 2023. These changes were not new national laws. They were choices made by Experian, Equifax, and TransUnion. These choices help many people because medical bills can appear without warning or clear details. These changes are still in place today.

The first change is that paid medical collection debts are not shown on credit reports. If you once had a medical bill in collections but later paid it, the credit bureaus remove it. The second change is that medical collection debts under five hundred dollars are not shown. These small debts no longer affect your score. The third change is that a medical collection debt cannot be added to your credit report until one full year has passed. This gives you time to work with doctors, hospitals, and insurance before a bill becomes a problem.

Even with these protections, some medical debts can still appear on credit reports. If a medical bill is large, unpaid, and more than one year old, and if it has been sent to a collection agency, it may still be shown. This is because federal law allows credit reporting companies to show accurate information unless a rule blocks it. The Fair Credit Reporting Act does not ban medical debt from reports. It only requires that the information be accurate and complete.

There was a major national discussion about medical debt reporting in 2024 and 2025. Federal consumer officials proposed a rule that would have removed medical debt from credit reports. This rule did not go into effect. Because it never became active, the rules around medical debt are the same as before. The credit bureaus still follow their voluntary policies. Larger medical debts can still be reported if they are accurate.

Your rights under the Fair Credit Reporting Act have not changed. You still have the right to see your credit report in full. You still have the right to dispute anything that looks wrong. You still have the right to request proof of a debt. If a medical debt shows up, the steps are simple. Ask the provider or the collection agency for an itemized bill. Compare their records with your own. Look at dates, amounts, and insurance payments. Errors in these areas are common.

If something does not match, you can dispute the item with the credit bureau. You can send a letter that explains the problem and attach any papers that support your claim. The credit bureau must investigate. If they cannot verify the debt with clear records, they must remove it. This part of the law is strong and gives you real control.

If the medical bill is valid and you owe it, there are still steps you can take. You can talk to the provider or the collector and ask for a payment plan. Ask for clear terms in writing. Do not agree to anything you cannot afford. Slow, steady payments can keep the situation from getting worse. Keeping records of every payment and letter helps protect you.

Medical bills are stressful. They often come from illness, injury, or moments you did not plan for. The credit system does not always reflect that reality. Still, you have tools that help you stay safe. You can check your reports often. You can dispute errors. You can ask for proof. You can correct wrong information. You can protect your score even when medical debt feels overwhelming.

This chapter gives you the facts you need for 2026. It shows what medical debt can be reported and what cannot. It shows what the bureaus have removed. It shows your rights under federal law. It gives you a plan that is simple and steady. You are not powerless in this process. You can take clear steps to protect your credit and your future.

10

How Auto Loans, Leases, and Dealership Inquiries Affect Your Credit in 2026

Auto loans are one of the biggest forces in a modern credit report. They build credit fast, damage credit fast, and confuse millions of consumers every year. Few people understand how dealership financing works, why so many inquiries appear at once, or how an auto loan can raise a credit score faster than a credit card. This chapter is your complete guide to how auto financing impacts your credit in 2026, including what to do, what not to do, and what to avoid at all costs.

Auto financing touches three major areas of the credit system. It matches real search demand, it follows real credit reporting behavior, and it reflects the newer 2024 to 2026 policy changes that affect how lenders process applications. Because of that, auto loans remain one of the most important lessons for anyone building or rebuilding credit.

Many people search for answers about auto credit every single month. They want to know if an auto loan helps a score. They want to know if leasing builds credit. They want to know why a dealership pulled their credit fifteen times. They want to know how to remove these inquiries. They want to know why their auto loan increased their score even before they made a payment. They want to know the safest way to get a car with bad credit. This chapter answers every one of those questions in simple and clear language so you never feel confused again.

Many people do not realize that dealerships routinely send your application to ten to twenty lenders in minutes. This is called rate shopping, but dealerships often do it without warning you. Each lender performs a separate hard inquiry. Every inquiry lands on your credit report. When ten or more appear at once, your score can drop. This is avoidable. This is the number one credit mistake consumers make every year. You will learn how to prevent this with simple steps that protect your score before you walk into any dealership.

Pre approval is the safest way to control how many lenders pull your credit. A pre approval from your bank or credit union sets a limit on how many inquiries can happen. It shows the dealer that you already have financing. They can still try to beat the rate, but they cannot shotgun your application without your permission. This chapter teaches you how to get a pre approval, how to present it at a dealership, and how to decline unnecessary credit pulls.

Auto loans build credit faster than credit cards because they are installment accounts. Installment loans help balance your credit file. They give you a mix of credit types which is an important factor in credit scoring. When you open a new auto loan, your score may rise because you now have a fuller profile. This can happen even before your first payment posts. For people rebuilding credit or starting from scratch, an auto loan can be one of the fastest ways to create a healthy file.

This chapter explains the difference between leasing and financing. A lease is reported the same way as an auto loan. It creates a real tradeline, builds payment history, and helps your credit mix. The main difference is that you never own the car. When you finance, you are building an installment loan that ends with ownership. Both build credit. Both can help your score. Both can damage your score if you miss a payment.

Many people do not understand installment utilization. With credit cards, utilization is the ratio of your balance to your limit. With auto loans, your balance naturally decreases over time. As your loan gets smaller, your score can rise. This is why many people see their score improve after twelve to eighteen months of steady car payments. This chapter explains how installment utilization works and why paying down your auto loan early must be done carefully. Paying it too fast can reduce your credit mix and lower your score. Paying it slowly and methodically helps your score grow.

Late payments on auto loans are serious. A credit card late payment hurts your score. A late auto loan payment hurts even more because car loans are seen as core financial obligations. The credit system assumes that people pay their car notes before anything else because a car is needed for work, daily life, and emergencies. When an auto loan is late, the scoring models assume deep financial stress. This is why even one late payment can drop a score more than a late credit card payment. This chapter teaches you how to avoid lates, how grace periods work, and how to talk to your lender before a late is reported.

Refinancing can help reduce your interest rate if your credit score has improved since your original loan. Many people refinance their auto loans after twelve months of payments. When you refinance, the old loan closes and a new loan appears. This can temporarily drop your score because of the new inquiry and the loss of age on the old account. Over time, the savings from a lower rate can outweigh the temporary drop. This chapter shows you how to refinance safely, when it makes sense, and how to choose lenders that do not abuse hard pulls.

Repossession is one of the hardest credit events. When a car is repossessed, it is reported as a severe delinquency. A voluntary repossession does not protect your credit score. Both voluntary and involuntary repossessions are reported the same way. After a repossession, the balance that remains after the car is sold often shows up as a collection or charge off. This chapter explains repossession reporting, how deficiency balances work, and what rights you have under federal law to dispute incorrect or duplicate reporting.

This is the definitive guide for what to do and what not to do in 2026. You will learn how to control your inquiries, how to prevent shotgun applications, how to talk to a dealer, how to read your auto loan tradeline, how to protect your score during refinancing, how to manage your installment utilization, how many points a late auto payment can drop your score, how negative events like repossessions and deficiency balances report, and how to dispute auto loan errors with precision.

Auto loans will always be one of the biggest factors in your credit profile. When you understand how they work, you can use them to your advantage. You can build fast. You can avoid traps. You can protect your score. And you can move through the process with confidence instead of fear. This chapter gives you everything you need to succeed.

11

How SBA EIDL and PPP Loans Show Up on Credit Reports

Many people took government backed loans during the COVID years. These loans helped small businesses and workers stay afloat. The two most common loans were the Paycheck Protection Program loan, called the PPP loan, and the Economic Injury Disaster Loan, known as the EIDL loan. Even though these loans came from the Small Business Administration, they do not follow the same rules as personal credit cards or personal loans. This chapter explains what is known and confirmed about how these loans may affect personal credit reports in 2026.

PPP loans were created to help businesses keep paying workers during the hardest part of the pandemic. PPP loans were designed to be forgiven if the borrower followed the rules. Forgiven PPP loans do not appear on personal credit reports because they are treated as forgiven debt for the business. When a PPP loan is forgiven, it is cleared and does not damage personal credit. Public information shows no reporting of forgiven PPP loans to the major credit bureaus.

EIDL loans were meant for very small businesses and self employed people who needed extra support. These loans were not forgiven unless the borrower received a separate advance. EIDL loans are business loans. Most EIDL loans do not appear on personal credit reports because credit bureaus do not list business debt on personal files unless the borrower signed a personal guarantee and the loan went into serious default. This is stated in public SBA guidance and in credit bureau policies.

If an SBA loan goes into default, the government can take steps to collect the debt. These steps may include sending the debt to the Treasury Offset Program. If the debt is sent to collection, it may appear on a personal credit report, but only if the loan is tied to the individual and if the reporting is accurate. Not all SBA debt is reported to credit bureaus. Whether it appears depends on the type of loan and the borrower's role in the business. What matters most is whether the person signed a personal guarantee and whether the loan was left unpaid.

If an SBA debt shows up on your credit report and you believe it is wrong, you can dispute it under the Fair Credit Reporting Act. The rules are the same as any other debt. You can ask the credit bureau to investigate. You can ask the SBA or the collection agency for records. You can compare the information on the report with the loan documents you have. If the information is wrong or missing, you can request a correction. If the debt cannot be verified, the credit bureau must fix it.

If the SBA debt is correct and you owe it, the safest step is to contact the SBA or the collection agency and ask what options you have. You may be able to set up a payment plan. The SBA also has hardship programs for some situations. Paying the debt or setting up a clear plan can help prevent further problems. Keeping copies of every letter and email can protect you if you need to dispute something later.

Many people worry that SBA loans will ruin their credit. In truth, most PPP and EIDL loans do not appear on personal credit reports. They may affect your business, but they do not always affect your personal file. Personal credit damage usually happens only when a loan is tied to the individual and the debt is unpaid. If you stayed current or received forgiveness, your credit is protected.

This chapter gives you clear steps to understand what can and cannot show up on a personal credit report when dealing with SBA loans. It gives you the facts that can be confirmed today, so you can protect your credit and plan your next steps with confidence.

12

How Tax Debt Affects Your Credit

Many people worry that unpaid taxes will destroy their credit. The truth is simple. The Internal Revenue Service does not report tax debt, payment plans, or audits directly to the three major credit bureaus. This rule protects your privacy and comes from federal law. Your credit report will not show that you owe back taxes, that you are on a payment plan, or that you filed your taxes late.

In the past, federal tax liens were public records, and credit bureaus sometimes added those liens to personal credit reports. That changed in 2018 when the three major credit bureaus stopped including tax liens in personal credit files. This is confirmed in public announcements from the credit bureaus. Today tax liens do not appear on personal credit reports. A lender may still find a tax lien by searching public records on their own, but it will not appear on your Equifax, Experian, or TransUnion file.

Your credit can still be affected by unpaid taxes, but not in a direct way. The IRS may take steps to collect the debt if it remains unpaid. These steps may include freezing a refund, placing a levy on wages, or placing a levy on a bank account. A levy is a legal action the IRS can take to collect a tax debt. A levy does not show up on a credit report. The indirect impact comes from the strain the levy may place on your finances. If a levy causes you to miss payments on other debts, those missed payments can hurt your credit.

If you owe taxes, the safest step is to contact the IRS early. The IRS offers payment plans called Installment Agreements. These plans allow you to make monthly payments until the debt is paid off. When you enter a payment plan and stay current, the IRS will not place a levy on your wages or bank account. This keeps the debt from affecting your other bills and protects your credit.

If you cannot pay the full amount, you can ask the IRS about an Offer in Compromise. This program lets some taxpayers settle for less than the full amount owed. The IRS reviews your income, expenses, and ability to pay. If approved, you can settle the debt and move forward. An Offer in Compromise is not reported to credit bureaus. Your personal credit report will not show that the offer happened.

If the IRS sends a debt to a private collection agency, the rules stay the same. The private collector cannot add the tax debt to your credit report. They can only try to collect the debt. If they report anything to a credit bureau that is not allowed, you can dispute it under the Fair Credit Reporting Act. A credit bureau must correct information that is wrong or not allowed.

Tax debt can feel stressful, but it does not directly damage your credit score. What matters most is how you manage the situation. Calling the IRS early, setting up a payment plan, and keeping records protects your finances. When you understand these facts, you can handle tax debt with less fear and keep your credit strong.

13

Buy Now Pay Later in 2026, How Klarna, Afterpay, and Affirm Really Affect Your Credit

Buy Now Pay Later services grew into a quiet financial habit for millions of people, and by 2026 the ripple effects of these small payments have become impossible to ignore. Companies like Klarna, Afterpay, Affirm, PayPal Pay in 4, MyPay from Chime, Empower Loans, and dozens of newer BNPL start ups promise instant approval, fast checkout, and no traditional credit check. People use them for sneakers, electronics, concert tickets, beauty products, groceries, and almost everything else. It feels harmless in the moment. It feels like free money. The truth is more complicated, and the credit impact in 2026 is finally becoming visible.

The biggest shift is that the Consumer Financial Protection Bureau has placed BNPL companies under the same federal supervision as traditional lenders. This means their reporting habits, their late fee structures, and their customer data practices are no longer operating in a gray zone. It does not mean that every BNPL payment is now guaranteed to appear on your credit report. What it means is that these companies can no longer operate without clear rules, and those rules are tightening every year.

Most BNPL companies still do not report on time payments to the major credit bureaus. This is important to understand. You can make fifty perfect BNPL payments and your score may not go up at all, because the bureaus may not be receiving that data in a way that fits the current scoring models. The scoring systems used by the major bureaus were not originally designed to handle short, four week repayment plans. They were built around longer installment loans. Until the models change, on time BNPL payments often vanish into the background.

Where BNPL becomes dangerous is in the late and missed payments. This is where the reporting does happen, and where the damage becomes real. If you miss multiple payments with Affirm, Klarna, Afterpay, PayPal Pay in 4, MyPay from Chime, Empower, or similar services, the account can be sent to a third party collector. The collection agency is the one that reports the debt to the credit bureau, and that negative mark hits your report like any other collection account. It can drop a score by many points, and the emotional shock often comes from the small size of the debt. It surprises people to learn that a forty dollar BNPL purchase can lead to a collection account that lingers for years.

Another hidden issue is stacking. BNPL companies approve accounts quickly and without long applications. As a result, many people juggle multiple BNPL plans across several apps. One payment is due on Tuesday, another on Friday, another next week, and another the week after that. It feels manageable until your paycheck changes or your bank account dips. What looks like four tiny payments becomes a tangled web that is easy to lose track of. This is how many users fall into accidental delinquency.

New models are being tested to include BNPL data in credit reports, but the rollout is slow. Some BNPL companies have experimented with reporting certain long term installment plans to the major bureaus, usually the plans that include interest. These reports do not always show up consistently, and the bureaus handle them carefully because older scoring models cannot interpret them cleanly. The industry is still figuring out how to incorporate this data without punishing consumers unfairly.

MyPay from Chime and Empower Loans add another wrinkle. These services sit between traditional BNPL and short term installment lending. They may include soft checks, early access features, or cash flow based underwriting. The goal is to make borrowing fast and convenient, but the repayment behavior still matters. Missed payments can be sent to collections, and the collection accounts will appear on your credit report even if the original loan did not.

As regulators move toward standardized reporting for BNPL, the industry is preparing for the next stage. The trend in 2026 is clear. The federal government is pushing BNPL companies toward transparency, predictable fees, clearer disclosures, and responsible credit practices. The next step will likely include unified credit reporting rules so that lenders can see a complete picture of a consumer's borrowing behavior. Until that happens, BNPL sits in a strange middle space. It does not fully build credit, but it can absolutely damage it.

Consumers should approach BNPL as a real loan, even if the company markets it like a lifestyle upgrade. If a bill can create a collection account, it is a serious bill. If a missed payment can trigger outside collections, it deserves the same attention you would give a credit card or a car loan. The safest path in 2026 is to keep BNPL use limited, organized, and intentional. The convenience is real, but so are the consequences.

BNPL is not evil, and it is not a trap. It is simply a form of credit that matured faster than the rules surrounding it. As the rules catch up, you will see more reporting, more clarity, and more accountability. Until then, treat each BNPL plan as a financial commitment. Keep the payments visible. Do not stack too many. Never assume that a missed BNPL payment disappears. It rarely does. And if you choose to use these services, use them with the full understanding that you are borrowing money. The more clearly you see that truth, the safer your credit will be.

14

EBT, SNAP, and Government Benefits: Do Credit Checks Matter

Disclaimer: *This chapter sits alongside the federal policy sections because EBT, SNAP, and similar government programs often appear in the same searches as student loans, medical debt, and tax debt. These programs do not report to credit bureaus, but consumers regularly ask how their eligibility interacts with credit checks, so this chapter answers those specific concerns clearly.*

People often worry that bad credit will affect their ability to receive government support. In 2025 and 2026, this is one of the most searched questions online because of misinformation and panic around changes to federal programs. The truth is simple. Standard credit checks are not used for SNAP benefits, commonly known as EBT, or for most public assistance programs. These programs are based on income, household size, and eligibility rules set by federal and state agencies. Your credit score does not determine whether you qualify.

SNAP, Medicaid, and most housing programs use financial verification, not credit scoring. They check income, employment, bank statements, and residency documents. They do not need your credit score to determine eligibility. The confusion comes from the fact that some agencies use identity verification tools. These are not credit checks. They confirm who you are, not whether you pay your bills on time.

There are a few exceptions. Certain housing authority programs may run a limited check to see if there is eviction-related debt owed to a government housing agency. This is not a full credit score pull and does not affect your score. It does not report to your file. It is only used to verify whether you owe the agency money.

Some people believe that EBT or SNAP benefits will decline if they have debt or collections. That is not true. These programs do not use credit scores in any part of the decision. Your score does not raise or lower your benefit amount. Your eligibility is based entirely on income guidelines.

Even though benefits do not use credit scores, rebuilding credit still matters. When your credit improves, you gain access to safer financial tools, better rates, and more stability. Government benefits may help with food or healthcare, but credit helps with long-term freedom. You can work on both at the same time without conflict.

15

What You Should and Should Not Dispute

You have the right to dispute any item on your credit report that is wrong, incomplete, or cannot be verified. This right comes from the Fair Credit Reporting Act. The law is simple. Every item on your report must be accurate. It must be complete. It must be able to be proven by the source that reported it. If any part of the information is wrong, you can dispute it. If the source cannot prove the information, the credit bureau must correct it.

You should dispute an item when the dates do not match the real payment history. You should dispute an item when the balance on the report is not the balance shown in your own records. You should dispute accounts that do not belong to you. You should dispute mixed information from someone else with a similar name. You should dispute duplicate accounts. You should dispute older accounts that are past the legal reporting period. These types of mistakes are common and can be fixed through the dispute process.

You should also dispute an account when you have proof that the information is not correct. For example, if you paid a debt and the report still shows it as unpaid, you can use your records to request a correction. If a collector reports a debt that is outside the time period for reporting, you can dispute it. The normal time limit for most negative information is seven years from the original date of delinquency. If the dates on the report are outside that window, you can ask for removal.

You should not dispute an item when the information is correct. Disputing accurate negative items does not help you. It can slow down your progress and can trigger extra checks. The credit bureaus must keep correct information on your report, even if it is negative. Late payments, charge offs, and collections that reflect real history cannot be removed just because they hurt your score. The dispute system is designed to fix mistakes, not to erase accurate history.

You should not dispute an account again and again when you have already received a complete and correct response. Repeated disputes of the same item can be marked as frivolous. If a bureau labels a dispute as frivolous, they do not need to reinvestigate. This does not harm your score, but it wastes time. The safest path is to dispute only when you can point to an actual error or a missing detail that needs correction.

You should not dispute an account that you know is valid simply because someone online said it will be removed. Many people online claim that all items can be deleted. This is not true. The law only requires the credit bureau to fix errors and remove items that cannot be verified. If the debt is real, the lender can verify it, and the account will stay. Trying to force the removal of correct information is not a real credit repair strategy.

You should not dispute identity related items unless they are wrong. Your name, your address, and your job information do not affect your score. They do not change approval odds. You only need to fix them if they belong to someone else or if they were added by mistake. Fixing old addresses can help organize your report, but it does not raise your score by itself.

The safest way to approach disputes is simple. Pull your real reports. Compare each line with your own records. Mark what is wrong. Submit clear disputes with clear evidence. Keep copies of everything. When you follow this method, you fix real mistakes and avoid problems that come from disputing items that are already correct.

A good credit report is an accurate credit report. The goal is not to erase the past. The goal is to make sure the information that shows up is correct and can be proven. When you focus only on the items that are truly wrong, you protect your progress and save time. This is the best way to repair your credit and keep your file clean.

16

How to Write an Effective Factual Dispute Letter

A factual dispute letter is the safest way to fix mistakes on your credit report. This type of letter tells the credit bureau or the furnisher exactly what is wrong, why it is wrong, and what proof you have. Federal law gives you this right (Consumer Financial Protection Bureau, 2018).

Start your letter with your full name, address, and any identifying information the bureau or furnisher needs, such as your Social Security number, date of birth, or account number. This helps them match your request to the correct file. The CFPB sample layout shows this format clearly (Consumer Financial Protection Bureau, 2018).

Identify the account you dispute using the account number or other identifying detail. If the lender has multiple accounts under your name, this step ensures they check the right record (Consumer Financial Protection Bureau, 2018).

Then explain clearly what is wrong. For example, state that the balance on the report does not match what you have paid; or, that the account is not yours; or, that the dates of delinquency are wrong; or, that the account was paid long ago (Consumer Financial Protection Bureau, 2018).

Attach proof. Include copies of receipts, statements, payment confirmations, or any document that supports your claim. Do not send original documents. If you include a copy of your credit report, circle the disputed items (Consumer Financial Protection Bureau, 2018).

If you have more than one item to dispute, list each separately as Dispute 1, Dispute 2, etc. This helps the bureau review them one by one without confusion (Consumer Financial Protection Bureau, 2018).

At the end, sign the letter and keep a copy for your records. This creates a paper trail in case you need to follow up. A clear paper trail helps protect your rights if the bureau does not respond properly (Consumer Financial Protection Bureau, 2018).

Federal law requires credit bureaus and furnishers to investigate disputes that are clear, specific, and supported by evidence (Fair Credit Reporting Act, 15 U.S.C. § 1681i). When your letter follows this structure, the bureau must complete the investigation. If the furnisher cannot verify the item, they must remove or correct it.

A factual dispute letter works because it follows both the federal law and the consumer-guidance standards. It does not try to erase valid history. Instead, it forces the system to check its facts. When you write clearly and provide proof, you protect your rights and give yourself the best chance of correcting errors.

17

Sample Credit Dispute Letter for 2026 (Factual, Legal, and Easy to Customize)

Disclaimer: *This sample dispute letter is provided for educational purposes only. Dispute letters must always be tailored to the exact errors on your credit report. A one size fits all or blanket template should never be used because it can cause investigations to be rejected. This example simply shows the structure of a proper factual dispute. You must replace every bracketed section with the real account information, dates, facts, and documentation from your own report.*

CFPB SAMPLE DISPUTE LETTER (EDUCATIONAL EXAMPLE)

[Your Name]
[Your Current Address]
[City, State ZIP Code]
[Email Address]
[Phone Number]
[Date]

[Company Name]
[Company Address for Direct Disputes]

Re: Request for Investigation and Correction of Inaccurate Credit Reporting

To Whom It May Concern,

I am contacting you to request a full investigation into inaccurate information that appears under your company's name on my consumer credit report. The details below are taken directly from the report so the correct account can be located.

Disputed Item 1

- Account Number: [Insert number or identifying details]
- Reported Date or Status: [Insert the date or status as it appears on the report]
- Reason for Dispute:

[Provide a clear explanation. Examples include:
 – The balance reported is incorrect based on payments already made.
 – The date of first delinquency is not accurate.
 – The account shows a late payment during a period when I was enrolled in a payment plan.
 – I do not recognize this account and believe it may be related to identity theft.]

Disputed Item 2 (If Applicable)

- Account Number: [Insert details]
- Reported Date or Status: [Insert details]
- Reason for Dispute: [Explain clearly]

If helpful for your review, I have included a copy of the relevant page of my credit report with the disputed items marked for easy reference. I have also included any supporting documents available.

I respectfully request a reinvestigation in accordance with the Fair Credit Reporting Act and a correction of any information found to be inaccurate or incomplete. Please provide written confirmation once your review is complete.

Thank you for your time and attention.

Sincerely,

[Your Name]

ChatGPT Prompt

18

Hard Inquiry Disputes

Hard inquiries confuse many people because they look small, but they can affect your score more than you expect. A hard inquiry appears on your report when a lender checks your credit for an application you submitted. Most lenders pull your file when you apply for a card, a loan, or financing. A single inquiry has a small impact, but multiple inquiries clustered together can make lenders think you are seeking credit aggressively or dealing with financial stress.

Hard inquiries stay on your report for two years, but they only affect your score for the first twelve months. You have the right to dispute a hard inquiry only when the inquiry is not yours. The reporting rules are strict. You cannot remove an inquiry that resulted from an application you actually submitted, even if you later changed your mind. You can only challenge inquiries that were unauthorized, fraudulent, or created because a company pulled your credit without your permission.

Many people discover unauthorized inquiries when they face identity theft, mixed files, or dealership practices where an application is sent to several lenders at once. Auto dealerships and mortgage brokers often send your application to many banks. The credit system groups mortgage and auto inquiries within a short window, but the impact can still feel heavy. You protect yourself by asking for the name of the bank that will run your credit and confirming whether more than one pull will occur. You protect yourself by getting preapproved by your own bank before walking into a dealership.

When you dispute an unauthorized inquiry, you follow the same factual method you learned earlier. You state that you did not authorize the inquiry. You explain that you never applied with the company listed. You ask for deletion under the Fair Credit Reporting Act. You attach any proof showing you did not submit an application. If the furnisher cannot prove that the pull was legitimate, the inquiry must be removed. This is your right, and it is one of the simplest ways to clean your file when you face identity theft or false activity.

Hard inquiries rarely stop someone from rebuilding. They matter less than utilization, payment history, and the amount of positive credit you build. When an inquiry is accurate, you do not waste energy trying to remove it. When it is not yours, you use the law with calm and precision. You take control of your report and move forward with clarity.

19

What Happens After You Dispute

When you send a dispute, the credit bureau must begin a process called reinvestigation. This is your right under federal law. The bureau must review the information you sent and then contact the company that reported the item. The law says the bureau must complete the reinvestigation within a set period of time (Fair Credit Reporting Act, 15 U.S.C. § 1681i).

The bureau forwards your dispute to the furnisher. The furnisher is the company that reported the information. This may be a lender, a collection agency, or a bank. The furnisher must check its records. It must look at the details you provided. It must compare its records with the claim you made. If the furnisher sees that the information is wrong, it must correct it. If the furnisher cannot prove that the information is right, it must update or remove the item (Fair Credit Reporting Act, 15 U.S.C. § 1681i).

If the furnisher confirms the information, the credit bureau updates the report. If the furnisher changes the information, the bureau must also update your file. If the furnisher cannot verify the information, the bureau must delete it or correct it. These steps protect you and keep your credit report accurate.

When the reinvestigation is complete, the bureau must send you the results in writing. The results tell you if the item stayed the same, changed, or was removed. If a change was made, the bureau must give you a free updated copy of your credit report (Consumer Financial Protection Bureau, 2018).

Sometimes a credit bureau may mark a dispute as frivolous. This happens only when the bureau believes you did not provide enough information or when the dispute repeats the same claim without new details. If a bureau marks a dispute as frivolous, it must tell you. It must explain why it made that decision. It must tell you what information you need to provide to continue the process (Consumer Financial Protection Bureau, 2018).

A frivolous label does not hurt your score. It only stops the reinvestigation. You can fix this by sending a clearer dispute with more detail or with better documents. When you provide the needed information, the bureau must move forward with a real investigation.

If you disagree with the results of a reinvestigation, you can add a statement to your credit report. This is called a consumer statement. It lets you explain the dispute in your own words. While a consumer statement does not change your score, it can help explain the situation to a lender reviewing your file.

The most important thing to remember is that the dispute process is built to protect accuracy. When you send a clear and complete dispute, the law gives you a fair review. The bureau must check your claim. The furnisher must check its records. If anything cannot be proven, it must be corrected. When you understand these steps, you can move through the dispute process with confidence.

20

How to Use the CFPB Complaint System

The Consumer Financial Protection Bureau gives you one of the strongest tools in credit repair. This tool is free. It is federal. It is public. And it forces companies to respond to you. When a bureau, collector, or furnisher refuses to correct something that is clearly wrong, the CFPB complaint system becomes the pressure that moves the process forward.

A CFPB complaint is not a dispute. It is a formal report to a federal agency saying that a company failed to follow the law. Many consumers use this when bureaus ignore their letters, when collectors do not validate debts, or when companies mark accounts incorrectly. The CFPB sends your complaint directly to the company you named. That company must respond. Most responses arrive within fifteen days, and most cases close within sixty days.

You use the CFPB complaint system when you have proof of an error, when you have already disputed with the bureaus, and when the company failed to correct the mistake. You upload your letters. You upload your proof. You explain what happened in simple language. You do not exaggerate. You do not stretch the truth. You present the facts and allow the law to work.

People often feel nervous when filing a complaint because they think they are starting a fight. In reality, you are simply using your federal rights. The

CFPB exists to protect you. It exists to hold companies accountable. It exists to collect data on patterns of misconduct. The system is designed to help you when you cannot move forward alone.

A CFPB complaint can help when a bureau lists the wrong balance, wrong date, or wrong creditor. It can help when a collector reports a debt without validation. It can help when an account you closed shows as open. It can help when a company continues to update an account even after it was deleted from your report.

You do not file complaints for small issues. You use it when something matters and when the dispute process failed. You use it with care. You use it with respect for the truth. And when you use it properly, it becomes one of the most powerful steps in the entire repair system.

21

Collections, Charge Offs, and Pay for Delete Truths

A collection is a debt that was not paid on time and was sent to a collection agency. A charge off is when a lender writes a debt off as a loss. A charge off does not mean the debt is forgiven. The lender can still try to collect it or sell it to a collector. These events can appear on your credit report because the Fair Credit Reporting Act allows lenders to report accurate account history (Fair Credit Reporting Act, 15 U.S.C. § 1681c).

When a collection agency contacts you, it must follow the rules set by the Fair Debt Collection Practices Act. This law explains what collectors can and cannot do. Collectors cannot mislead you, threaten you, or call you at unreasonable hours. They must tell you basic information about the debt. You have the right to ask for written validation, and they must provide it (Fair Debt Collection Practices Act, 15 U.S.C. § 1692g).

You can dispute a collection if it is wrong. If the amount is not correct, if the dates do not match your records, or if the debt does not belong to you, you can dispute it with both the collector and the credit bureau. When you dispute an item, the credit bureau must investigate, and the collector must review the information. If the collector cannot verify the debt, it must be corrected or removed (Fair Credit Reporting Act, 15 U.S.C. § 1681i).

A collection stays on your credit report for up to seven years from the original date of delinquency. This timeline is set by federal law (Fair Credit Reporting Act, 15 U.S.C. § 1681c). Paying a collection does not erase the record. It only updates the status to paid. The record stays until the reporting period ends.

Some collectors may agree to delete a collection after full payment or settlement. This is known as pay for delete. Credit bureaus do not require collectors to delete paid collections. It is a voluntary choice. Some collectors offer it, and some do not. The bureaus allow deletion if the furnisher requests it. There is no federal rule that bans it or guarantees it. You can ask a collector if they offer deletion, but they do not have to say yes. If they agree, you should request the terms in writing before you pay.

If a collector offers a settlement, you should ask for a clear letter that lists the amount, the due date, and whether the account will be closed or updated. If the collector agrees to delete the account after payment, you should get that in writing. This protects you if the collector does not update the report correctly.

You should be careful not to restart an old debt by making an unplanned payment or agreeing to new terms. Some states have laws called statutes of limitation. These laws limit how long a collector can sue you for a debt. If you make a new payment or promise to pay, you may restart the time period. The credit reporting period does not restart, but the legal collection period might. You should check your state laws or speak with a qualified advisor if you are unsure.

Paying or settling a collection can help your financial stability. It can stop calls and prevent legal action. It can help you qualify for housing if the collection is tied to a rental debt. It can help you move forward. But payment alone does not remove the record from your credit file unless the collector chooses to delete it.

The safest path with collections is simple. Check your credit reports. Compare the reported details with your own records. Dispute any errors. Ask the collector for written validation. Request a written agreement before you pay. Keep copies of everything. When you follow these steps, you protect your rights and keep your credit report accurate.

22

Why a 7-Year-Old Debt Still Shows Up: Statute of Limitations vs. Credit Reporting Rules in 2026

Many people feel confused when they see an old debt still sitting on their credit report. They think, "This debt is so old. Why is it still here?" The problem is that two different clocks control debt. One clock controls how long a debt can be collected. The other clock controls how long a debt can appear on your credit report. These clocks do not match, and this is why old debt still shows up.

The first clock is called the statute of limitations. Every state has its own time limit for how long a company can sue you to collect a debt. In some states it is three years. In others it can be up to six years or more. When this time ends, the debt becomes too old to collect in court. This does not erase the debt. It only stops lawsuits. A collector can still try to contact you, but they cannot take you to court once the time runs out.

The second clock is the credit reporting time limit. This is a federal rule. It comes from the Fair Credit Reporting Act, which says most negative accounts can stay on your report for up to seven years from the date you first fell behind.

This seven year rule does not change based on your state. It does not follow the statute of limitations. It stands on its own.

This means a debt can be too old to collect but still appear on your credit report. For example, a credit card in a state with a three year statute of limitations can no longer be collected after three years. But it can still stay on your report for seven years from the first time it was late. This gap makes people think something is wrong when it is actually how the law works.

Collectors know this gap well. Some will try to get you to make even a small payment. One payment can restart the statute of limitations in many states. This gives them more time to sue you. This is called re-aging a debt. You avoid this by not paying an old debt until you know the rules of your state. When you talk to a collector, you also avoid admitting the debt. You keep the conversation simple. You ask them to verify the account. You do not restart the clock by accident.

There is also another problem. Some collectors sell old debts again and again. Every time a new collector buys the debt, they may report it to the credit bureaus. If they change the date of first delinquency, this is a violation. The date of first delinquency must stay the same. You can dispute wrong dates and get them corrected or removed. When the date is fixed, the seven year countdown is clear.

Understanding the two clocks helps you protect yourself. A debt can stop being collectible after a few years. It can still stay on your report until seven years pass. These rules do not depend on how the debt feels. They follow the law. When you know the law, you avoid fear and confusion.

When you see an old debt on your report, you check two things. First, you check the date of first delinquency. This tells you when the seven year credit rule will end. Second, you check the statute of limitations in your state. This tells you if the debt can still be collected. When you know both, you can make safe choices.

If the debt is too old for court and close to the seven year removal date, you often leave it alone. If the date looks wrong, you dispute it as inaccurate. If a collector tries to push you into a payment on a very old debt, you use your rights. You do not restart the clock.

Credit repair becomes easier when you understand these basic rules. Old debt has limits. It has timelines. It cannot chase you forever. You learn what must stay and what must go. You learn when to dispute and when to wait. You learn when a collector has power and when they do not.

You are not stuck. You have rights. And when you understand these two clocks, you stay safe, calm, and in control of your own credit story.

23

Credit Freezes, Fraud Alerts, and Identity Protection in 2026

Identity theft is one of the fastest-growing causes of credit damage today. A single fraudulent account can lower your score, trigger collection calls, and force you into long disputes. This chapter shows you how to protect yourself before problems start and how to secure your credit file after you repair it.

A credit freeze is the strongest tool you have. A freeze blocks lenders from pulling your report unless you lift it. When your file is frozen, no one can open credit in your name. You can still dispute errors, access your reports, and use your existing accounts. The freeze only stops new accounts from being approved. In 2026, freezes remain free under federal law at all three bureaus: Equifax, Experian, and TransUnion.

A fraud alert is a lighter form of protection. When you place a fraud alert, lenders must take extra steps before approving credit. They may call you or require extra ID. Fraud alerts do not block new accounts, but they slow down approval and make it harder for thieves to use your information. A standard fraud alert lasts one year and can be renewed. An extended alert lasts seven years if you have an FTC identity theft report.

Credit monitoring is useful but not enough by itself. Monitoring tells you when something changes, but monitoring does not stop the change from happening. You always want a freeze in place unless you are actively applying for credit. Many banks now offer free monitoring tools. You can also use government resources like IdentityTheft.gov to create reports, track cases, and get step-by-step identity recovery plans.

If you believe someone used your Social Security number, you need to freeze your reports immediately, pull all three reports from AnnualCreditReport.co m, and check for accounts you do not recognize. Any unauthorized account should be disputed in writing. If the account is confirmed as fraud, you can use the FTC identity theft report to force deletion under federal law. This is explained in the next chapter.

Freezing your secondary bureaus is also helpful. Fraudsters sometimes target smaller bureaus that store your address history, phone numbers, public records, or identity-linked data. Freezing LexisNexis and SageStream adds extra layers of protection. These bureaus are often used to verify identity when new credit is opened. When they are frozen, thieves have a harder time passing identity checks.

A freeze does not harm your score. It does not lower your points or affect your creditworthiness. It simply locks the door. When you need to apply for credit, you can lift the freeze temporarily using a PIN or login. Once the lender completes the pull, you can refreeze it the same day.

If you receive collection calls for accounts you did not open, do not ignore them. Ask for written validation. Pull your reports again. Fraud often spreads because thieves try multiple applications once they get one approval. Early detection prevents damage and saves months of disputes later.

Identity theft often happens after a data breach. Large companies and government agencies face constant attacks, and millions of Social Security numbers have already been exposed in the last decade. Freezes turn those stolen numbers into dead ends.

A freeze is also important after you finish repairing your credit. When your score rises, you become a more attractive target. Thieves tend to avoid frozen files because they cannot open new accounts without going through extra steps.

If you have been through financial trauma or have struggled with lost mail, unstable housing, or shared living environments, freezes and alerts give you a sense of control. They protect your progress and keep your file clean while you rebuild.

A freeze is simple, safe, and effective. A fraud alert adds protection for times when you cannot freeze. Identity monitoring helps you stay aware of changes. Together, these tools keep your credit stable in a world where identity theft is common.

Your credit file is one of your most valuable assets. Lock it. Guard it. Protect it.

24

Identity Theft, Fraud, and Guaranteed Federal Deletions

Identity theft happens when someone uses your personal information without permission. This can include opening accounts in your name or making charges you did not approve. Federal law gives you strong protections when this happens. These protections come from the Fair Credit Reporting Act and from federal identity theft rules. When you follow the steps in this chapter, you can force the credit bureaus to remove fraudulent accounts.

The first step is to file an identity theft report. You can file this report with the Federal Trade Commission at IdentityTheft.gov. The FTC gives you an official identity theft affidavit after you complete the report (Federal Trade Commission, 2023). This affidavit is accepted by credit bureaus and by many lenders. It helps you prove that the account was not yours.

The next step is to send the identity theft documents to the credit bureaus. You include your FTC report, your affidavit, your ID copy, and a letter that explains which accounts are fraudulent. The Fair Credit Reporting Act says the bureaus must block any information that came from identity theft when you give them an identity theft report and proof of your identity (Fair Credit

Reporting Act, 15 U.S.C. § 1681c-2).

When the bureau receives your identity theft report, it must block the fraudulent account from your credit file. This block must happen within a short time period. The block stops lenders from seeing the fraudulent account. If the account appears again, you can send the report again and request another block. The block must stay unless the bureau finds that the report was false or incomplete.

You can also send the identity theft documents to the lender or collector. When they receive your identity theft report, they cannot continue reporting the account as yours. They must stop furnishing the information to credit bureaus. They must review their records to confirm that the account was created by fraud. If they cannot prove that you opened the account, they must remove it from their reporting (Fair Credit Reporting Act, 15 U.S.C. § 1681c-2).

You should also place a fraud alert with the credit bureaus. A fraud alert tells lenders to take extra steps before opening new accounts. A fraud alert is free and lasts one year. You can renew it. You can also freeze your credit. A freeze stops new accounts from being opened until you lift it. A freeze is free and does not affect your score (Consumer Financial Protection Bureau, 2018).

If a fraudulent account caused a collection or a charge off, you can dispute those items too. You send the same identity theft documents to the collector and to the bureau. You explain that the account was created without your permission. Under federal law, the collector must stop reporting the account if it is tied to identity theft (Fair Credit Reporting Act, 15 U.S.C. § 1681c-2).

You should keep copies of everything you send. Keep your FTC report. Keep your letters. Keep your ID copies. These records protect you if a lender or bureau needs more information later. Identity theft cases can take time, but the federal rules are clear. Fraudulent accounts must be blocked. Fraudulent accounts must be removed when you provide the right documents.

When you follow these steps, you use federal law to protect your credit. You do not have to live with accounts that someone else created. You do not have to explain charges that were not yours. The law helps you clear your report and move forward with confidence.

25

Specialty Consumer Reporting Agencies and How They Affect Your Credit

The Hidden Architecture of Credit Reporting

Most people think credit reporting begins and ends with the three major bureaus. The truth is that many smaller agencies collect and share data that can influence your credit checks. These agencies do not give you a score, but they hold information that lenders use to confirm your identity and your history. They are called **specialty consumer reporting agencies**. All of them must follow the Fair Credit Reporting Act. This means they must give you a copy of your file when you ask, and they must let you place a freeze to block new access.

LexisNexis is one of the largest data companies in the country. It stores public records, identity information, and background information. Lenders sometimes use it to confirm that your name, address, and Social Security number match. It does not set your score, but it can influence how lenders verify your identity.

Innovis is a consumer reporting agency that works alongside the major bureaus. It does not always appear in credit repair guides, but it provides data used for identity checks and account verification. You can request your Innovis report for free. You can freeze it to block new access.

SageStream is another consumer reporting agency. It collects identity and behavioral information. It is now operated by LexisNexis. Some lenders use it when they review new credit applications. Freezing SageStream can limit access to this data during certain types of checks.

CoreLogic runs several specialty databases, including rental history and mortgage related information. It can hold records on evictions, tenant screening, and other housing related checks. These records do not change your credit score. They can be used when you apply for housing or mortgage loans. You can request your file and freeze it.

ChexSystems is used by banks to track checking account history. If you had problems with overdrafts or unpaid bank fees, these records may appear in ChexSystems. Banks use this system to decide whether to open a new checking account. You can dispute errors and freeze this file under the same federal rules that apply to the credit bureaus.

ARS, also known as Advanced Resolution Services, helps lenders verify identity and application data. It does not produce a traditional credit report. Lenders use it to compare your information with public and private databases. You can request your file and freeze it like the others.

These agencies are part of the ***hidden structure behind*** the major credit bureaus. When a credit bureau checks your dispute, it may use some of these sources to confirm your identity or to verify information about an account. When you freeze a specialty agency, the flow of data is limited. This does not force a specific outcome, but it can affect how easily a lender or bureau can check your information.

You can protect yourself by pulling your files from each agency. You can check for errors and dispute anything that is wrong. You can freeze each agency to control access to your information. Every freeze is free. Every file disclosure is free. These steps give you more control over the data that lenders use during credit checks.

When you understand these agencies, you understand a major part of the credit system that most people never see. This knowledge gives you more control and protects you when you are repairing your credit.

26

Authorized User Tradelines and Business Tradelines in 2026, What Helps, What Hurts, and What to Avoid

Authorized user tradelines have been part of the credit industry for decades, yet most people have only heard about them through rumors or fast credit repair promises. In 2026, the interest in tradelines is rising again because lenders, influencers, and BNPL companies have created new pressure points that make people want faster improvements. There is a safe way to use authorized user accounts, and there is a dangerous way. This chapter explains both so you can avoid traps and use the strategy correctly.

An authorized user tradeline is simple on paper. Someone with a strong credit card adds you to their account, and their history appears on your credit report. If the account is old, clean, and low in utilization, you may benefit from the added age and stability. It does not always raise the score by hundreds of points the way some companies promise, but it can help when the profile is thin, when there is limited credit history, or when your own past includes long gaps with no open accounts.

The benefit comes from the credit card's age, payment history, and balance behavior. If the card is older than your accounts, your file gains more age. If the payment history is spotless, your file gains a layer of reliability. If the utilization is low, your file looks healthier. This is why parents often add their children to their cards. It is also why a partner may help a spouse rebuild after a setback. These are the natural and safe uses of an authorized user tradeline.

The problem begins when companies sell tradelines to strangers. Many people do not know that the credit industry monitors this practice closely. The companies offering rental access to someone else's account often charge a fee to add your name for two or three months. The account owner gets paid, and the buyer receives temporary credit history until the cardholder removes them. While the practice is not illegal on its face, the federal agencies view it as high risk because it can be used for fraud or score manipulation. Many lenders treat these rented tradelines with suspicion, especially if there is no relationship between the parties. Some lenders disregard them completely during underwriting.

In 2026, the safest approach is to use authorized user tradelines only when a real relationship exists. A parent, spouse, sibling, or trusted friend can add you to an account with a clean history. If the credit card issuer reports authorized user accounts, the benefit may appear within one or two reporting cycles. You never need to use the physical card. You never need to have access to the credit line. The purpose is history and stability, not spending.

If the account has late payments, high balances, or recent delinquencies, it can harm your score. You must review the account in detail before agreeing to be added. You want an account that has years of perfect history and a balance that stays comfortably low. If the owner of the account struggles with their payments, their struggles will become your struggles. The risk moves with the relationship.

Business tradelines sit in a different category. Many companies claim they can sell business credit tradelines to help a new company qualify for loans. The marketing sounds similar to personal tradeline sales, but the risk in business credit is even higher. Business credit reporting agencies operate differently from personal bureaus. The scoring models are not identical to FICO. They weigh payment behavior more heavily and rely on past activity with vendors and lenders.

Some newcomers believe that buying business tradelines will allow them to secure high limit cards or large loans quickly. This is not realistic. The lenders who offer serious business credit, including banks and corporate issuers, often verify the legitimacy of business activity. They look for revenue, financial statements, tax filings, and actual trade history. A purchased business tradeline that does not reflect real business transactions can be ignored during underwriting. In some situations, it can trigger review flags that slow down or deny applications.

The safer approach is to build business credit through real accounts. This begins with opening a business bank account, obtaining an EIN, and establishing a small number of vendor accounts that report to the major commercial bureaus. When these accounts are paid on time, the score grows naturally. This does not require large spending. It requires consistency and visible activity. Over time, lenders gain confidence in the business and gradually offer higher limits and better terms.

There is a temptation to search for shortcuts in both personal and business tradelines, especially when the repair process feels slow. It is important to remember that tradelines are tools, not miracles. They enhance an already improving credit report. They do not erase collections or undo late payments. They do not replace the core habits that shape your financial future. They give your file more depth, but they must be used with precision.

When used properly, authorized user accounts can help rebuild confidence. They can help you break the psychological weight of starting from zero.

Business tradelines based on real activity can help your company gain momentum. But neither should be used in isolation. They work best when they sit on top of clean reports, low balances, and a steady pattern of on time payments.

In 2026, the credit world rewards transparency, stability, and real behavior. Lenders want to see who you are financially, not who someone else is. If you choose to use authorized user tradelines, use them because the relationship makes sense. If you choose to build business credit, use real vendors and real transactions. When you move with honesty, the credit system responds more predictably. Your future will feel stronger because you built it on real steps instead of temporary signals.

27

How Long Credit Repair Really Takes

People search every day for one answer: how long does credit repair take. There is no single timeline because every credit profile holds different issues. Some people only need to dispute a handful of errors. Others are carrying years of late payments, high balances, and old collections. What you can expect in 2026 is simple. The more you follow a structured plan, the faster the repair.

Here is how credit repair usually moves when done correctly.

If your main issues are small errors, old dates, incorrect balances, duplicated accounts, or unverifiable information, the dispute process often shows results within thirty to ninety days because the bureaus are required to reinvestigate within thirty days once they receive your letter. Deletions happen when the furnisher cannot verify the information. If a furnisher responds quickly, the dispute may close faster.

If your main issues are high credit card balances, the changes can be even quicker. Utilization is one of the fastest scoring factors to react. When you lower balances before the statement closes, you often see improvements within one to two cycles. This is one of the fastest legal ways to raise a score.

If you are dealing with old debt, you need more time. Collections older than two years often have less impact on a score, but they still affect mortgage underwriting. If the information is accurate, you cannot delete it with a dispute. You can try a pay for delete arrangement with a collector. A pay for delete is a private agreement where a collection agency removes the reporting after payment. Not every collector offers it, but many do. When they remove it, the score responds quickly because the negative item disappears from the file.

If your biggest problem is late payments, the timeline is longer. A late payment stays for seven years. The impact fades over time, but the recent ones hurt the most. You cannot delete a legitimate late payment through a dispute. You can ask for a goodwill adjustment if you were historically a good customer. You can focus on rebuilding through utilization and new positive accounts while the late payment ages.

If your profile is severely damaged with multiple defaults, charge-offs, and years of missed payments, the repair becomes a longer project. Many people rebuild from this position within twelve to eighteen months through a combination of disputes, utilization control, secured cards, builder loans, and consistent payment history. You do not need to wait seven years for a new life. You need clean habits and time for new positive data to outweigh old damage.

If you are recovering from bankruptcy, the timeline depends on your rebuilding plan. Bankruptcy stays on your report for seven to ten years depending on the type. Even so, most people can return to the "good" range within two to four years if they rebuild aggressively with secured cards, low utilization, and no missed payments. Bankruptcy does not freeze your life. It resets it.

Credit repair moves as fast as your accuracy and consistency. You cannot rush the law, but you can move with the law. Your reports improve when the data improves. Scores rise when the pressure in the file falls. When you focus on factual disputes, low utilization, and steady payments, your timeline becomes predictable.

28

What Is a Good Credit Score in 2026

A credit score is a simple number with a complicated impact. It can open doors or close them. It can lower the cost of your life or raise it. It can shape the interest you pay, the apartment you qualify for, the insurance rates you receive, and the credit limits that lenders trust you with. In 2026, the meaning of a "good" credit score has shifted slightly because lenders are more cautious after the pandemic, the student loan restart, and increased consumer defaults. Knowing the ranges and knowing what lenders look for saves you time and frustration.

The most common score used in the United States is the FICO Score. The ranges stay the same:

- 300 to 579 is considered poor
- 580 to 669 is considered fair
- 670 to 739 is considered good
- 740 to 799 is considered very good
- 800 to 850 is considered exceptional

What matters more than the number is how lenders interpret risk in a changing economy. A 700 score in 2026 is not viewed the same as it was in 2018. Lenders want stability. They want low utilization. They want no recent late payments. They want clean reports. They want fewer inquiries. This means you may qualify for the same approvals as before, but lenders now look deeper at your entire report before approving credit or setting rates.

A "good" score does not guarantee the best terms if your balances are high or if your recent history shows strain. A "fair" score does not block you if your profile shows stability and low utilization. The score is one piece. The report is the full picture. Your goal is not perfection. Your goal is a score that gives you access and a file that makes lenders feel safe. Most people can reach the "good" or "very good" range with low utilization, consistent payments, and the dispute methods in this book.

Your score is not fixed. It reflects the last few months of your financial behavior. When you change your habits, the score follows. When you lower balances, the score reacts. When you add new positive accounts, the score rises again. A good score is simply a stable score. It is within reach for anyone who follows the steps in this book.

29

How to Build Positive Credit the Smart Way

A strong credit score needs positive account history. Deletions help when something is wrong, but they do not build the foundation of your score. The simplest way to raise your score over time is to add new accounts that report on time. These accounts show lenders that you can borrow and pay back money in a steady way. When you build this kind of history, your score can grow even if you had problems in the past.

A secured credit card is one of the easiest tools. A secured card uses a deposit as the credit limit. You make the deposit, you use the card for small purchases, and you pay the balance on time. The card reports your payments to the credit bureaus. After several months of on time payments, your score can begin to rise. Some banks may return your deposit later and turn the card into a regular account.

Credit builder loans also help. These loans work in reverse. The bank or credit union holds the loan amount in a savings account. You make monthly payments until the amount is paid off. When you finish, the money is released back to you. Each payment builds positive credit history. These loans are often small and easy to manage.

Some financial apps offer credit building programs. Chime has a credit builder account that uses a secured structure. Self offers a credit builder loan with an app that guides your payments. These tools work because they report steady payments to the credit bureaus. They do not fix negative items on their own. They simply add new positive history that helps raise your score over time.

An authorized user account can also help. This happens when someone adds you to a credit card with a good history. When the card reports to the credit bureaus, the positive history may appear on your report. This can help you if the account has low balances and a long history of on time payments. Not all lenders treat authorized user accounts the same way, but many do include them in credit scoring.

Small lines of credit offered by some apps or banks may also help. Some companies offer small spending limits that report as credit accounts. These lines can help build history when used carefully. The key is to keep the balance low and pay on time.

Positive credit grows over months, not days. Every on time payment adds strength. Every low balance helps your score. If you add two or three positive accounts and manage them well, your report begins to tell a new story. Lenders like to see steady behavior more than any other factor.

You should avoid opening too many accounts at once. Opening too many new accounts can make your report look unstable. One or two accounts is enough to begin rebuilding. The goal is not to collect credit. The goal is to build trust.

You should check your statements and pay them on time every month. A single late payment can slow your progress. A missed payment can hurt your score. When you pay on time and keep balances low, you show lenders that you can manage credit safely.

Building credit is simple when you follow these steps. Add a secured card. Add a credit builder loan. Use small limits. Pay everything on time. Keep balances low. Over time your report will show positive history, and your score will grow. This is the safest and most reliable way to rebuild credit.

30

Utilization: The Fastest Legal Score Booster

Credit utilization is the amount of credit you use compared to the amount you have. It is one of the biggest parts of your credit score. When your balance is high, your score can drop. When your balance is low, your score can rise. This can happen fast because utilization updates every time your lender reports your balance to the credit bureaus.

Every credit card has two important dates. The first date is the due date. This is the day you must pay to avoid a late fee. The second date is the statement closing date. This is the day your lender reports your balance to the credit bureaus. Most people pay only on the due date. This protects them from late fees, but it does not always help their credit score. What matters most is the balance on the statement closing date.

You can lower your score by lowering your balance before the lender reports it. If you pay down your card right before the statement closing date, the lower balance is the one that is sent to the credit bureaus. This lowers your utilization and may help your score rise. This simple timing change can help you make progress even if you cannot pay the full balance all at once.

If you have a limit of one thousand dollars and you owe nine hundred dollars, your utilization is very high. This can pull your score down. If you pay the balance down to one hundred dollars before the statement date, the lender will report the lower balance. This can help your score move up in a short time. The same is true with several small payments. Paying once in the middle of the month and once near the closing date can keep your balance low when it is reported.

You do not need to bring every card to zero. You only need to keep your balances low on the reporting day. A card with a small purchase that you pay off often can help your score. A card with a high balance near the limit can hurt it. If you have several cards, spreading purchases across them can keep each balance low. This prevents one card from showing high use.

If your balances are high on all cards, focus on lowering one card at a time. When one card drops, your total utilization drops. This can give you a score increase even when the other cards still have balances. It can also help you feel more in control. You do not need to fix everything at once. One card at a time is enough.

You can also ask your bank for a higher credit limit. If the bank approves, the new limit can lower your utilization even if the balance stays the same. This helps only if you do not spend the new limit. A higher limit with the same balance can lower your percentage.

It is best to avoid closing old cards. When you close a card, you lose its credit limit. This can raise your utilization and lower your score. Keeping old cards open, even with no balance, helps keep your total credit limit higher. This makes it easier to keep utilization low.

Utilization changes because lenders report every month. This is why lowering balances before the statement closing date is the fastest score booster for most people. You do not need a long time to see progress. You only need to control the balance that gets reported. When you understand how utilization works, you can use it to build your score in a safe and steady way.

31

Rent, Utilities, and Phone Bills: Turning Everyday Payments Into Credit in 2026

Rent, utilities, and phone bills are some of the most consistent payments people make, yet most of them do not show up on a traditional credit report. In 2026, alternative data is becoming more common, and many people are using it to strengthen their credit profile. When these payments appear in your file, they help you build a longer and more consistent payment history, especially if you have a thin credit file.

Rent reporting is one of the most powerful tools. It appears as a rental payment tradeline on your report and shows your on-time housing history. FICO and VantageScore models can use this information, and it can help many people increase their score over time. Rent is not as strong as a mortgage or a major loan, but it carries more weight than utilities or streaming services.

To use rent reporting, you need a company that sends your monthly payments to the bureaus. The most reputable and widely used rent reporting companies include:

1. Rent Reporters

Website: rentreporters.com

Rent Reporters verifies your lease with your landlord and reports your monthly payments to TransUnion. They are known for being beginner-friendly and have strong customer service.

2. Boom Pay

Website: useboom.com

Boom reports rent to all three major credit bureaus. They also offer past rent reporting, which can give you instant history if your payment records qualify.

3. LevelCredit

Website: levelcredit.com

LevelCredit reports rent and utilities to TransUnion and Equifax. It is well-known for being affordable and simple for renters who want consistent monthly updates.

These companies do not create negative history unless your landlord confirms a missed payment during verification. You remain in control of what gets added to your file, and you decide whether to continue reporting each month.

Utility and telecom reporting also help, although they carry less weight in scoring models. Many platforms will report electric, gas, water, phone, and internet bills. These records appear as alternative data, and they help show that you pay your major monthly responsibilities. The most reliable tools include:

1. **Experian Boost**
   Website: experian.com/boost

Boost connects to your bank account and pulls utility, telecom, and streaming payments. It updates your Experian score and allows you to remove any service that reports late.

2. **LevelCredit Utility Reporting**
   Website: levelcredit.com

LevelCredit reports eligible utility bills to the bureaus and keeps the reporting positive. Missed payments are not added unless they eventually become collections.

3. **Grow Credit**
   Website: growcredit.com

Grow Credit uses a small loan structure to report on-time payments for phone bills, streaming services, and subscription-based apps. These payments appear as a credit account rather than a utility tradeline.

Alternative data has limits. FICO models weigh rent more than utilities, and utilities more than streaming. Rent builds the most consistent history. Utilities help if you have a thin file. Streaming offers almost no score impact on its own. These tools work best when combined with secured cards, builder loans, and low credit card balances.

If you choose to use alternative reporting, you want to keep your payments steady. You want to avoid late payments. You want to be sure the service only reports on-time history and allows you to opt out of anything negative. Many people use rent reporting as a bridge to new credit. They start with six or twelve months of rent history. Then they add a secured card. Then they keep their balances low. Little by little, the score rises.

Alternative data does not replace traditional credit, but it helps people who need a fresh start. It helps people who are rebuilding. It helps people who do not qualify for regular credit cards yet. In 2026, these tools are becoming more common, and more lenders pay attention to them. When you pair them with the rest of your credit repair plan, they help you move forward with confidence.

If you stay consistent with your rent, utilities, and phone bills, these tools can turn everyday life into a path for rebuilding. They give you a chance to show responsibility in a system that does not always acknowledge it. Used wisely, they become a quiet but steady way to strengthen your credit profile.

32

Debt Stress, Financial Trauma, and Money Clarity

Debt does not only affect your money. It affects your mind and your body. When you are stressed about bills, your nervous system reacts. Your heart can beat faster. Your thoughts can speed up. You may feel pressure in your chest or stomach. You may feel fear when you check your bank account. This stress can make money choices harder. It can make simple tasks feel heavy.

When you feel this stress every day, you can enter a cycle. You avoid opening bills. You delay looking at your credit report. You ignore letters from lenders. You say you will deal with it later, but later never comes. This cycle is common. It does not mean you are lazy. It means your body is trying to protect you from something that feels painful.

Financial trauma happens when money problems repeat over time. This can come from job loss, eviction, childhood poverty, past debt, or growing up in a home where money was always scarce. When this happens, the brain can link money with danger. Even small money decisions can feel unsafe. You may feel tired, angry, or shut down when you try to deal with debt.

When you understand that these reactions are normal, you can begin to take steps that bring calm and clarity. The first step is to breathe and slow down. You do not have to fix everything in one day. You only need one calm moment to start. When you check your report, you do it with care, not panic. When you look at your bills, you do it without rushing. Slow steps help your mind feel safe.

The next step is to break your money tasks into small pieces. You do not need to think about everything at once. You only need to pick the next small action. One small action could be pulling your credit report. Another action could be checking one account on that report. Another action could be writing down one balance. When you do small steps, the stress becomes less sharp.

You can also protect your mind by using simple routines. You can check your accounts on the same day each week. You can pay one bill at the same time each month. Routines help your nervous system feel safe because they create order. When money becomes predictable, the stress becomes smaller. This makes it easier to make good choices.

When you begin to understand your reactions, you will notice patterns. Maybe you worry most at night. Maybe you avoid mail. Maybe you feel fear when a number looks bigger than you expected. These patterns do not make you weak. They show you where to add structure and calm. When you add structure, your brain feels safer, and your choices become clearer.

Money clarity does not come from being perfect. It comes from being steady. It comes from small steps taken again and again. When you take these steps, your credit decisions become easier. Your thinking becomes sharper. You feel more in control. Debt loses its power when your mind feels calm enough to deal with it.

This chapter is not about blame. It is about understanding yourself. When debt no longer feels like danger, you can move forward. You can read your report. You can make a plan. You can take real steps. You can rebuild. Your past choices do not control your future. Your new calm will guide you.

33

Negotiating With Creditors Like a Professional

When you talk to a creditor, the words you choose matter less than the calm you bring into the call. Creditors deal with stress every day, and most people speak fast, panic, or apologize too much. You do not need to do any of that. You only need to be clear, steady, and in control of your information.

The first step is to know the details of the account before you speak to anyone. Write down the balance, the account number, the dates, and the last payment you remember making. When you know your facts, you do not feel rushed on the call. You can take your time. You can answer or decline to answer without fear.

When the creditor asks for information, you give only what is needed to identify the account. You do not tell stories. You do not explain your life. You do not argue. You stay focused on the present. When the creditor talks, you listen first, then respond slowly. This keeps the call steady and removes tension.

When you want to settle or reduce a balance, you speak in simple terms. You explain what you can pay, not what you wish you could pay. Creditors respond better to clear numbers. You can say that you want to resolve the account for a smaller amount. You can also ask which options are available. When you ask calmly, you open more doors.

If the creditor offers a plan, you do not agree on the spot. You write it down. You read it back to them to confirm it. You ask them to send everything in writing before you pay anything. This protects you. When the terms are in writing, the creditor must follow them. Without written proof, nothing is guaranteed.

You must avoid restarting old debt by mistake. If an account is very old, a small payment or a promise to pay can restart the timeline for collection. This is called the statute of limitations. The rules depend on the state, so you avoid making any promise until you know how old the debt is. When you are unsure, you do not agree to anything on the call.

Phantom debt collectors are another danger. Some companies chase debts that are not real or not owed by you. When a collector cannot clearly identify the original creditor, the full balance, or the dates, you end the call. You do not argue. You do not explain. You simply say you want the details in writing. If they refuse, you do not continue speaking with them.

You can negotiate from a position of strength even when you owe money. Creditors want resolution. They want payment. They want a clear end to the account. When you stay calm, take notes, repeat details back to them, and ask for everything in writing, you show that you are serious and organized. This helps the conversation move in your favor.

You do not need perfect language to negotiate. You only need patience, clarity, and slow steady speech. You control the pace of the call by taking your time. When you do this, you think better, and you protect yourself from mistakes.

Every agreement must be in writing before you send money. Every number must match what you discussed. Every rule must be clear.

This is how professionals negotiate. It is also how you protect your future.

34

The Truth About 609 Letters and Why 611 Is What Matters

Many people online claim that a 609 letter can delete anything from your credit report. This is not true. Section 609 of the Fair Credit Reporting Act is real, but it does not create a right to delete negative items. Section 609 is about your right to access information that the credit reporting companies hold about you. It does not force removal of accurate information.

Section 609 says that credit reporting companies must give you the information in your file when you request it. The law states that the agency must "clearly and accurately disclose to the consumer all information in the consumer's file" (Fair Credit Reporting Act, 15 U.S.C. § 1681g). This tells us what the law is meant for. It confirms your right to see your data. It does not give you a deletion right.

Many websites have spread the idea that a 609 letter can delete any account by asking for the original contract. This is not what the law says. The law does not require furnishers to provide a signed contract to verify an account. It only requires the credit reporting company to share the information in your file. This is why 609 letters rarely lead to removal of accurate accounts. They are built on a misunderstanding of what the law covers.

The real power comes from Section 611. This section gives you the right to dispute information that you believe is inaccurate. When you dispute, the credit reporting company must investigate the claim. The law states that the agency must "conduct a reasonable reinvestigation to determine whether the disputed information is inaccurate" (Fair Credit Reporting Act, 15 U.S.C. § 1681i). This is the section that controls correction and deletion of errors.

Section 611 is what professionals use because it requires action. If the information cannot be verified, it must be corrected or removed. This is the path that works. You explain the problem. You provide documents when you have them. You send the dispute in writing so you have a record. The company then must investigate the dispute. This is the clean, lawful process that credit attorneys and consumer advocates follow.

When you understand the difference between these two laws, you make better choices. You do not waste time on forms that promise magic results. You do not follow myths that say any account can be deleted. You work with the law as it is written. You use Section 611 to challenge errors. You ask for corrections when the item does not match your records. You ask for removal only when the information cannot be verified or is wrong.

You are not required to use legal terms to dispute an item. You only need to be clear about the problem. When the information is wrong, you say why it is wrong. When the balance is incorrect, you show your records. When the account does not belong to you, you explain that. You keep your dispute simple and direct. This is what gets results.

When you build your system around verified rules instead of online shortcuts, you protect your time and your peace of mind. The law gives you real tools that work. Section 609 lets you see your data. Section 611 lets you correct your data. When you follow these rules, you move your credit forward with confidence.

35

Advanced Strategies for Significant Score Increases

you want a larger jump in your score, small changes are not always enough. You may need a set of steps that work together. These steps do not replace the basics. They simply add more power when used with clean reports, steady payments, and controlled balances. These strategies are real, safe, and used by people who need faster changes without tricks or false promises.

One helpful step is asking for early exclusion. This is when a credit reporting company removes an old negative item a few months before the seven year limit. Each company has its own timeline. Some may help you a few months early. Some may not. This step only works when the item is close to aging off. It does not work on new accounts. When you ask, you stay calm and simple. You only ask if the item is eligible for early removal based on age.

Another step is cleaning up old addresses. When your report has many past addresses, it can confuse the system. It can also make it harder to verify your disputes. When you remove old addresses that are not linked to open accounts, you create a cleaner file. You do not remove any address that is tied to an active loan or card. You only remove what is outdated or incorrect. A clean file helps future disputes move smoother.

Some people also choose to request removal of certain inquiries. This only works in limited cases. If the inquiry was caused by fraud or was placed by mistake, you can ask the credit reporting company to remove it. You cannot remove inquiries that you allowed. You cannot remove inquiries from shopping for credit. Only wrong or fraudulent inquiries can be challenged.

You can also combine bureau disputes with furnisher disputes. A furnisher is the company that gave the information to the credit reporting company. When you send a dispute to both places, you make each side check the records. You stay factual. You explain the problem. You include documents when you have them. This gives you a stronger chance for correction, because both sides must look at the details instead of only one.

Another helpful step is using a method of verification request when needed. This is when you ask the credit reporting company to explain how they verified the information after a dispute. You do not use this as a threat or shortcut. You use it only when a clear error remains and you need to understand how the company checked the details. This helps you decide your next move.

When you stack these strategies together, you can create larger changes in your score. Early exclusion removes old weight. Address cleanup reduces noise in your file. Inquiry removal clears errors. Combined disputes increase pressure for accuracy. When all of these steps support each other, your score can rise faster in a clean and lawful way.

You do not need to do all of these at once. You pick what fits your situation. You move slowly and keep notes. You stay steady each month. When you do this, you build a clear path to a stronger score without rushing or using shortcuts that do not work.

You are shaping your credit in a smart, careful way. This is how real progress is made.

36

The Top A+ Rated Credit Repair Companies of 2026 (Verified List + Websites)

People search for credit repair help more than almost any other financial topic. When someone types "best credit repair companies" into Google, they are usually tired, overwhelmed, or stuck. They want to know which companies are real, which ones follow the law, and which ones actually help you move forward. This chapter gives you a clear, factual, and transparent answer by listing the top A-plus rated credit repair companies recognized through public consumer reviews and long-standing industry presence. These are all companies that have been publicly referenced in verified lists, ranking articles, and Better Business Bureau reports. You should always verify current ratings and terms before signing up, but this chapter gives you a strong starting point if you need help beyond the DIY strategy taught throughout this book.

Credit repair companies cannot remove accurate negative information, and no company can guarantee deletions. What they can do is help you organize your disputes, communicate with furnishers, and manage the steps that feel overwhelming when you are exhausted, working long hours, or trying to recover from major financial stress. These companies follow structured dispute cycles based on the Fair Credit Reporting Act, and many people find them helpful when they need extra support.

Below are the companies you researched and verified from trusted online sources. Each has a long operating history and a clear service model. The descriptions that follow explain what these companies are known for, along with their official websites so you can review their terms directly.

Credit Saint is one of the most recognized companies in the field. They are known for a transparent dispute process, clear pricing, and long-term consumer satisfaction across many publicly posted reviews. Their site can be found at https://www.creditsaint.com.

Sky Blue Credit is well known for simplicity and affordability. They have a structured monthly process, a satisfaction guarantee, and a straightforward approach that many first-time rebuilders appreciate. Their official website is https://www.skybluecredit.com.

The Credit Pros blends technology with credit repair services. They offer dashboards, digital tools, and automated monitoring that help consumers track their progress. Many people choose them for convenience and organization. Their website is https://www.thecreditpros.com.

MSI Credit Solutions has built a reputation for active timelines and assertive dispute cycles. Consumers often mention strong communication and responsive service, especially for complicated files. Their website is https://www.msicredit.com.

Ovation Credit Repair, backed by LendingTree, offers structured plans and an easy onboarding process. Many people choose them because they feel safer working with a company under a large financial parent umbrella. Their website is https://www.ovationcredit.com.

The Credit People is known for a longer satisfaction guarantee than many competitors. Their plans are simple, and their customer service reputation is solid across multiple review platforms. You can learn more at https://www.thecreditpeople.com.

CreditFirm.net is a company that focuses on transparency. Their pricing is simple, and consumers often choose them because the terms feel straightforward and predictable. Their website is https://www.creditfirm.net.

Lexington Law is the most widely known credit repair service in the United States. They operate with paralegals under the supervision of attorneys, and they have worked with millions of consumers over many years. Consumers should review Lexington Law's current operational status, pricing, and compliance updates before enrolling, since the company has gone through various changes over time. Their website is https://www.lexingtonlaw.com.

In addition to traditional companies, there is a growing interest in AI-driven credit assistance. **DisputeBeast** is one example of a tool that uses artificial intelligence to help consumers draft letters, track their disputes, and organize their rebuild strategy. While it is not a replacement for legal advice, and while results vary based on the user's effort and accuracy, many people find AI helpful for managing large amounts of information. The DisputeBeast website is https://www.disputebeast.com.

These companies exist because credit repair can feel overwhelming when you are already under stress. Hiring a company may help when you feel emotionally drained or confused about the process. It can also help when your file is large, when you have many old accounts, or when you simply need a team to keep the dispute cycle moving every month. These services can offer structure, reminders, and a steady rhythm that is hard to maintain on your own.

There are also times when hiring a credit repair company is not the right move. If a company promises to remove accurate information, guarantees deletions, or claims they can erase your whole report, that is not legal. If a company pressures you or asks you to lie, walk away immediately. Ethical credit repair companies stay within the law. They use the dispute process properly, and they tell you the truth about what is possible.

A credit repair attorney may be a better option when you have identity theft cases, mixed files, stubborn uncorrected errors, or situations where a bureau fails to fix something after repeated disputes. Attorneys can apply legal pressure that standard companies cannot, especially when a furnisher refuses to correct something that is clearly wrong.

This chapter is placed in the advanced section of the book because by the time you reach it, you understand the laws, the dispute structure, the reporting rules, and the habits required for rebuilding. Now you can decide whether you want outside help or whether you feel strong enough to continue the process alone. Many readers use both approaches at different times in their journey.

No matter which path you choose, remember that no service; human or digital, can replace your long-term habits. Credit repair companies can dispute errors, but only you can protect your utilization, avoid late payments, monitor your accounts, and build new positive history. You are the architect of your future credit profile, and every step you take brings you closer to stability, confidence, and financial power.

If you choose to work with a company, verify everything independently, confirm current ratings, read the contracts carefully, and move only with services that follow the law and respect your rights. With patience, clarity, and solid information, you can rebuild your credit no matter where you start.

37

The Business Credit Masterclass for Entrepreneurs and Creators

When you start a business, you carry two credit lives. One is your personal credit. The other is your business credit. Both matter. Lenders look at your personal credit first because it shows how you manage money. They look at your business credit to see how your company handles its own bills. When both are steady, you gain access to larger lines, better rates, and more freedom to grow.

Your personal credit is the base. You want clean reports, on-time payments, and low balances. You want active accounts that show steady history. Lenders often use personal credit to decide if you can handle business credit. When your personal report looks strong, you stand out as a lower risk.

Once your personal credit is stable, you can begin building your business credit the right way. The first step is forming a real business structure. Many people start with an LLC. This gives your company its own identity that is separate from your personal life. Your business also needs an Employer Identification Number, called an EIN. This is like a Social Security Number for your company. You get it from the IRS at no cost. It helps lenders and suppliers track your business activity without using your personal Social

Security Number.

After you form your business and get your EIN, you can create your business credit file. Dun and Bradstreet is one of the main companies that tracks business credit. To start your file, you often need a DUNS number. This is the unique ID Dun and Bradstreet uses to build your business credit report. This report grows as you open accounts, make payments, and work with vendors.

Dun and Bradstreet uses a score called the Paydex score. This score measures how fast your business pays its bills. A high Paydex score means you pay early or on time. A low score means you pay late. Many lenders use the Paydex score to decide how much credit to give you. When you pay early, your score can grow faster. A strong Paydex score can help you get better terms and bigger lines as your business grows.

You can start building your business credit with small vendor accounts. These companies give starter lines for new businesses. They may let you buy supplies or simple items without requiring strong business history. When you pay them on time, they report your payments to the business credit agencies. This creates early positive history. Over time, these small accounts lead to larger vendor lines and business credit cards.

As your business grows, you may get access to higher credit limits. You may qualify for business cards that offer rewards or help with cash flow. These cards usually stay separate from your personal credit report when used with your EIN and proper business structure. This separation protects your personal score from large swings in business spending.

You can also use your personal credit to support your business in the early stages. When your personal report is strong, lenders may approve higher starting limits. These limits can help you handle early costs while your business credit file grows. You use these tools with care. You pay them down.

You avoid letting business expenses harm your personal credit.

Business credit grows faster when you follow simple habits. You check your balances. You pay your bills before they are due. You buy only what your business needs. You keep your structure clean. You maintain the same address, phone number, and bank account for your business. This consistency makes your business look stable in the eyes of lenders.

The goal of business credit is freedom. You want your company to qualify for lines, loans, and cards without relying on your personal credit. You want your business to stand on its own. You want your personal and business lives to support each other without mixing debts.

You do not need perfect credit to begin this path. You only need a steady base and simple habits. When your personal credit is clean and your business is set up the right way, your business can grow from month to month. You build trust with lenders. You open new doors. You create more space for your ideas to grow.

Your business becomes stronger when your credit system is organized and clean. This chapter gives you the tools to build both sides with clarity and confidence. Many creators begin with very little. They take small steps. They use what they have. They grow their credit life slowly. You can do the same. Your credit can support your ideas and help your business move forward one careful step at a time.

38

The 90-Day and Six-Month Credit Reset Plans

A credit reset does not happen in one day. It happens through slow and steady steps that build on each other. When you follow a plan, you take pressure off yourself. You stop guessing. You stop rushing. You focus on the next small action. When you stack simple steps, your credit begins to change. These plans give you calm structure so you can rebuild without fear or confusion.

This chapter gives you two paths. One is a 90-day plan. The other is a six-month plan. You can follow one or use both. Each timeline works with the way credit reporting companies update information. These plans help you clean errors, lower balances, create new positive history, and build habits that protect your score for life.

You do not need to be perfect. You only need to stay steady.

The 90-Day Credit Reset Plan

The 90-day plan is the fast path. It focuses on simple moves that can create meaningful change in a short time. This plan works when you want progress but do not want tricks or false promises. It gives you a clean start and leads into the longer plan if you want deeper changes.

Day One to Day Ten

You start by pulling your reports from AnnualCreditReport.com. You read each line slowly. You circle anything that looks wrong. You circle wrong dates, wrong balances, duplicate accounts, or accounts that do not belong to you. You do not rush. You simply mark what looks off.

You then remove old addresses that are not linked to active accounts. You ask the credit reporting company to update your personal information to reflect your current address. A clean personal file helps later steps move smoother.

You also freeze the secondary agencies. These include LexisNexis, SageStream, CoreLogic, ARS, and ChexSystems. When these agencies are frozen, your disputes move with less friction because fewer outside data points are used during checks.

Day Eleven to Day Thirty

You begin sending factual disputes for the items you circled. You write simple letters. You explain what the error is. You explain why it is wrong. You include a copy of your ID and proof of address. You do not include long stories. You stay calm and clear.

While you wait for the reinvestigation process, you focus on your balances. You aim to lower your utilization to ten to twenty percent. This is one of the fastest ways to move your score. You check when your card issuer reports to the credit reporting companies. You make a payment before that date so your lower balance is the one that gets reported.

You also add one positive account if you do not have many. This could be a secured card or a builder loan. You pick something you can manage with ease. You keep the balance low and pay on time.

Day Thirty-One to Day Sixty

You begin to receive responses from your disputes. Some items may be corrected. Some may be removed. Some may remain. If an error stays on your report and you have clear proof, you write a second factual letter. You stay patient. You keep copies of everything.

During this period, you keep lowering your balances. You avoid new inquiries unless the account will help you build history. You set a weekly check-in so you never feel lost or surprised.

This month is about steady movement. You are not chasing a number. You are building a clean foundation.

Day Sixty-One to Day Ninety

You read your updated reports again. You look at what changed. You look at what still needs help. If any items remain that are wrong or unclear, you can send a furnisher dispute to the company that supplied the information. You explain the same facts. You include the same proof.

At the same time, you continue your new positive account. You keep the utilization low. You stay away from late payments. You let the steps you already took begin to settle in your report.

By day ninety, you should see movement. You should see fewer errors. You should see lower balances. You should see early signs of score growth. The

90-day plan gives you direction. The six-month plan builds on it.

The Six-Month Credit Reset Plan

The six-month plan brings bigger changes. This plan takes you through deeper repair, stronger habits, and larger improvements. You build stability that stays with you long after the plan ends.

Month One

You follow the same steps from the 90-day plan. You clean your reports. You freeze the secondary agencies. You fix your addresses. You send your first disputes. You lower your balances. You set up one new positive account. You start your routine.

This month is the base.

Month Two

You check your reports again. You look at the results of your disputes. You correct anything that is still wrong. You write second letters if needed. You begin early exclusion requests for negative items that are close to aging off.

You focus on smoother money habits. You create one day each week to check in on your finances. You track due dates. You keep balances low. You build calm.

Month Three

You expand your positive credit. If you have only one new positive account, you add a second simple account. You pick something small that fits your income and comfort level. This helps your history grow faster and keeps your report balanced.

You look for any wrong inquiries. If you find inquiries caused by fraud or mistakes, you ask the credit reporting company to remove them. You only ask for removal when the inquiry is wrong.

This month is about expansion and cleanup.

Month Four

You check your reports again. You note every change. You note anything that still needs work. You keep all of your documents in one place. This helps you stay organized for the final steps.

If you have older collections that you want to settle, this is the time to negotiate. You never restart the debt by making promises without written terms. You only agree when the deal is in writing. You keep the settlement simple and clear.

Month Five

You focus on building your long-term habits. You pay everything before the due date. You keep your balance under twenty percent. You protect your accounts. You begin to shape your financial life with structure.

You look at your income and expenses. You make small changes that reduce stress. You avoid new debt that does not help you move forward.

Month Six

You take a full view of your credit. You look at where you started. You look at the steps you took. You look at the errors that were corrected. You look at your new accounts. You look at your lower balances.

You now have a cleaner, stronger report. You have new habits that protect you. You have structure that keeps you safe. You know how to handle your credit with confidence.

The six-month plan does not end here. It becomes your normal way of living. You are not crashing from crisis to crisis. You are steady. You are calm. You are rebuilding in a real and lasting way.

39

How to Prepare for Home Ownership

Buying a home is one of the biggest steps you can take with your credit. Lenders look at your full picture. They study your income, your debts, your history, and your habits. They want to see that you can handle a long future payment. When you understand how lenders think, you can prepare in a calm and simple way.

The first step is knowing your credit score range. You do not need a perfect score to buy a home. You only need a score that shows steady money habits. Many lenders approve buyers with a score that is good but not perfect. Your goal is to be stable. You want on-time payments, low balances, and a clean report with no open disputes. When your report looks steady, lenders see you as ready.

The next step is lowering your debts. Lenders look at something called your debt to income ratio. This is the amount you owe each month compared to the money you earn. When this number is lower, you look safer in the eyes of the lender. You can lower this number by paying down your cards and keeping your balances low. You also avoid taking new loans that make your monthly payments rise.

You also need savings. When you buy a home, you need money for your down payment, closing costs, and simple moving expenses. You do not need a huge amount. You only need enough to show that you can cover the early steps. Saving slowly each month helps you build this cushion. Even small savings help you reach the goal over time.

When your credit is clean and your savings grow, you can begin to look at loan programs. Many first time buyers use programs that make buying easier. These programs can help lower the down payment or give extra support. Some loans accept lower scores or lighter savings. Each program is different, so you choose the one that fits your life. You focus on steady monthly payments that you can manage without stress.

You also prepare your documents. Lenders will ask for pay stubs, bank statements, tax returns, and details about your debts. When you keep your documents in one folder, you move through the process with ease. This helps the lender understand your full picture in a simple way.

As you prepare, you check your report one more time. You make sure your name, address, and accounts are correct. You make sure all your disputes are closed. Lenders do not like open disputes because they change the score. A clean report gives the lender a clear view of your history.

The most important part of this process is patience. You do not rush. You do not panic if you see a number you do not like. You take one step at a time. You stay focused on your income, your debts, and your savings. When you follow this path, you move closer to owning a home without fear or confusion.

Home ownership is not about perfection. It is about preparation. When you care for your credit, protect your balances, stay steady with your payments, and save what you can, you open the door to a home that fits your life. You are building a safe place for your future, one calm step at a time.

40

The Free Credit Repair Plan That Actually Works

This is the free plan most people are really searching for. It does not use magic. It does not use lies. It does not use illegal tricks. It uses your legal rights, a clear routine, and a few smart moves that most people never learn. If you follow this plan with patience, your credit will start to change.

The first step is to pull all three of your real credit reports. You do this from the official site that gives you the full files from Equifax, Experian, and TransUnion. You download each report as a file so you can print them or mark them on your screen. You want the full details, not just a score from an app.

Once you have your reports, you read them line by line with a pen or highlighter. You circle anything that looks wrong, out of date, or out of place. You look for wrong balances, accounts you never opened, accounts listed twice, collections that should already show paid, items older than seven years, and hard inquiries you know you did not allow. You also look at the dates on late payments. If a late payment is listed in the wrong month, or the same late is shown twice, you mark it. These are the kinds of items that your legal rights actually support.

The next smart step is to freeze the specialty agencies that sit in the background. These are specialty and secondary consumer reporting agencies. They often hold public records, check writing history, banking records, and extra data that the big three companies use when checking your disputes. You contact agencies such as LexisNexis, SageStream or AAN, CoreLogic, Innovis, ARS, ChexSystems, and Clarity Services, and you ask for a security freeze on your files. This does not erase any debt. It does not change your past. It simply limits how much background data is pulled when someone tries to verify old information. When this extra data is locked, some items become harder to confirm and sometimes fall off when they cannot be fully supported.

Once that is in place, you choose what to dispute. You do not fight every negative item. You use a simple rule. If it is wrong, outdated, duplicated, belongs to someone else, or should not be there under the time rules, you dispute it. If it is a real debt that you know you owe and the details are correct, you do not use disputes as a game to make it vanish. You are playing chess, not chasing tricks. You remove what cannot be verified or should not be there. You leave honest history alone and handle it by payment, negotiation, or time.

Now you write factual dispute letters. You do not copy a random template someone posted online. Many of those are flagged and ignored. A strong letter is short and clear. You state who you are. You list the account you are talking about. You state exactly what is wrong. You explain what the correct information should be or that the account is not yours. You attach proof when you have it, like a payment receipt, a letter from a lender, or proof of address. You keep your tone calm. You are not begging. You are not yelling. You are simply asking for an accurate report as the law allows.

You send these dispute letters by mail, not through the quick online portals. When you use an app or site, you may agree to fine print that limits your rights. When you send letters by certified mail with tracking, you create a paper trail. You send one set to each of the three major companies for the items that appear on their reports. You keep copies of every letter and every green card or tracking slip.

After your letters arrive, a clock starts. The credit reporting companies usually have about thirty days to check with the company that reported the information. They ask whether the account and details can be confirmed. If the company cannot prove that the information is complete and accurate, the item must be corrected or removed. This is the heart of real credit repair. It is not instant. It is not dramatic. It is a system that forces old data to be checked and fixed.

While this process is running, you do something even more powerful. You build new positive history. You may open one or two simple accounts that you can handle without stress. This might be a secured credit card, a small credit builder loan, or a builder account from a trusted company. You also ask a trusted family member with a strong card and clean history if you can be added as an authorized user. You do not need to use their card. You only need to share their good history if they feel safe doing that for you. These simple moves add more fresh, positive lines to your report and can move your score over time.

You also work on your utilization, which is the share of your credit that you use. This is one of the most powerful score factors. A simple rule is to keep your reported balances around ten to twenty percent of your limits. If you have a three hundred dollar limit, you try to keep your balance near sixty dollars or less. The key hack is to pay your card down before the company reports to the credit reporting agencies, not just before the due date. This means the lower balance is the one they see, which helps your score.

There is another place where people can gain ground, which is debt negotiation. This only applies to real debts in collections. You pick a few important recent accounts that are less than a couple of years old and that you can afford to settle. You contact the collector and ask for an agreement where they will stop reporting the debt or update it to show it is no longer owed in exchange for payment. Some companies agree to a full removal. Some agree to update the status. You always get any deal in writing before you pay. You never give card or bank details until you have a written agreement.

As your disputes finish, you pull your reports again. You note which items fell off and which were corrected. You ask again to freeze the specialty agencies if any of them were unfrozen during the process. You add one or two more positive accounts only if your budget can handle them. You keep following the utilization rule. You protect your new on time payment streak like your life depends on it.

If you run into a stubborn error that stays after a dispute, you can use your deeper rights. You can ask the credit reporting company to show how they checked the information. You can send a dispute to the company that provided the data, and ask them to review their records. You can use your right to see information in your file when needed. The goal is not to become a lawyer. The goal is to use your basic rights when something is clearly wrong.

This free plan works because it is rooted in real law and real math. You fix errors. You make it harder for old unproven data to survive. You build fresh positive lines. You use your limits with care. You do not lie. You do not claim false identity theft. You do not use illegal numbers or fake files. You simply apply steady pressure and build new history. That is what the best credit repair attorneys and honest consultants do. You can do the same thing for yourself.

This is the real loophole. The loophole is not a trick. The loophole is that the system must follow rules, and most people never learn them. Now you know them. Your job is to apply them with patience and respect for yourself.

41

Bankruptcy, Rebuilding Credit, and Real Alternatives

Some people reach a point where the numbers do not work. The debts are too high. The income is too low. The calls do not stop. At that point, many people start to whisper one word to themselves. That word is bankruptcy. This word carries fear and shame for many people, but it is really a legal tool. It is serious and should never be taken lightly. It is also not the end of your financial life.

Bankruptcy is a court process that can erase or restructure certain debts. It is not a simple quick fix. It can sit on your credit reports for many years. It can make it harder to get new credit for a while. At the same time, for some people who are deeply stuck, it can be the reset button that allows life to go on. The key is to understand what it does, what it does not do, and what other choices you have.

There are two common types of personal bankruptcy. One is often called Chapter Seven. This type can wipe out many unsecured debts, such as credit cards and some personal loans, if you qualify. In exchange, some of your property may be sold to pay creditors, depending on the laws in your state and the amount of property you own. The other common type is often called

Chapter Thirteen. This is a repayment plan. In this type, you make regular payments over several years while protected from most collection actions. At the end of the plan, remaining eligible balances can be cleared.

Both forms of bankruptcy can remain on your credit reports for a long time. In many cases, a bankruptcy can appear for seven to ten years from the date you file. That sounds harsh, but the impact on your score generally softens as time passes, especially if you build good habits during those years. Many people have much better scores long before the bankruptcy disappears because they have learned to manage their credit with more care.

Before you reach for bankruptcy, it is wise to look at alternatives. One option is a debt management plan through a nonprofit credit counseling agency. In a debt management plan, an agency talks to your card companies and tries to lower your interest rates and create a set monthly payment. You make one payment to the agency, which then pays your creditors. This does not erase debt. It simply makes it more structured and often cheaper to carry. It can be a good fit if your income is stable but your interest costs are choking you.

Another option is direct negotiation. You can call your creditors and ask for hardship plans, lower interest, longer terms, or temporary pauses. Some creditors will work with you if you explain your situation and show that you want to pay. This is not always easy. It requires patience and calm communication. Still, many people have avoided default this way.

Debt settlement is another path, but it carries risk. In settlement, you or a company working for you tries to get creditors to accept less than the full amount. While you are waiting for deals, you may stop paying, which can lead to late marks, collection accounts, and lawsuits. Not all creditors agree to settle. Fees can be high. This path can damage your credit in the short term, even if it reduces what you owe. It is not a light choice.

If your debts are smaller and your income allows it, you may choose a slower self-directed payoff plan. You pick a method like the smallest balance first or highest interest rate first, and you attack one account at a time while paying at least the minimum on the rest. This is not fast or flashy, but it builds strong habits and protects your credit more than most other options.

If you and a trusted attorney decide that bankruptcy is the right move, the rebuilding process starts as soon as the case is filed. You begin by checking all three credit reports after the case is completed. You make sure that the accounts included in the bankruptcy show the right status. If there are errors, you dispute them with proof of your case details.

Next, you start building a new payment record. You make every remaining bill on time, every month. This includes rent, utilities, and any remaining loans. Over time, you may add a small secured credit card or a credit builder loan. You keep balances very low. You never pay late. Your goal is not to rush into large limits. Your goal is to show a long streak of calm, on time payments.

You also keep your new debts small. You do not finance things you do not need. You do not chase big car payments or large lines just to feel normal again. You accept that for a while, less is more. You give your credit time to heal.

Monitoring your reports once or twice a year becomes a normal habit. You watch for new errors. You correct them. You keep your utilization low and your payments steady. Over time, you may be surprised to see your score rise more than you expected. Many people see improvement within a couple of years after bankruptcy because they are finally able to keep up with their current bills and no longer carry constant late payments and collections.

Bankruptcy is not a shame mark on your soul. It is a sign that at one point, the numbers did not work and you chose a legal way to reset. Lenders will see it. You cannot hide it. But you can put strong behavior on top of it for many years. As those years pass, the bankruptcy becomes only one detail in a long story of better choices.

Whether you choose a debt management plan, careful negotiation, slow self payoff, or bankruptcy itself, the heart of your credit life remains the same. You protect your payment history. You keep your balances low. You avoid new trouble. You stay honest. You move at a pace that your nervous system and your income can handle.

Your credit story does not end with a crisis. It continues with the habits you build after the crisis. You always have the power to start that chapter today.

42

CASE STUDY: Rebuilding After Pandemic Hardship

This case study is about a man we will call John. He is fifty years old. Before the pandemic, his life felt stable. He worked at the same job for seven years. He paid his credit cards on time. His score was around seven hundred fifty. He did what people tell you to do. He built good credit. He trusted that if he did the right thing, the system would treat him fairly.

Then the pandemic hit. His job placed him on furlough. At first he hoped it would be short. He used his unemployment to keep every card current. He paid and paid, trying to protect his score. He did not know how long the crisis would last. When the unemployment ended, his employer did not bring him back. His income dropped to almost nothing. With no savings and no support, he hit a wall.

He missed his first payment. That first late payment was the first one in five years. It dropped his score from around seven hundred fifty to near six hundred. He felt shocked and angry. After all his hard work, his whole profile changed because he could not keep up during a once in a lifetime crisis. As time passed, late fees stacked up. His cards fell further behind. He stopped answering calls. His good credit life fell apart.

Now, years later, John's situation looks like this. He has an old Small Business Administration loan of about five thousand dollars on his report. He has a tax repair loan of about nine thousand dollars. He has around twenty five thousand dollars in credit card debt that has been delinquent for four to five years. He also owes about twenty thousand dollars to the tax authorities. His credit scores are in the low five hundreds. For a while he did nothing and let it all slide.

Recently, John's health has improved. He found work again. His income is not perfect, but it is steady. He is sober, clear, and ready to rebuild. This case study shows how someone like John can start over with a calm plan.

Step One: Face the Full Picture

The first step for John is to stop guessing and see the truth in writing. He needs to pull all three of his real credit reports from the official source and read them slowly. He prints them or saves them as files and marks every account, balance, and status. He writes down which debts are still with the original lender and which are now with collectors.

He also makes a simple list of all debts that do not show on his reports, such as any payment plan with the tax authorities. He notes the amounts, who he owes, and how old the debts are. This part is hard on the emotions, but it gives him back control. He moves from fear to facts.

Step Two: Sort Debts by Type and Risk

Once John has the full list, he sorts his debts into groups. One group is tax debt. Another is SBA debt. Another is his old credit cards and personal loans. Each group behaves in a different way.

Tax debts and SBA debts tend to have strong collection tools. They may lead to wage garnishment or other actions if ignored. Old credit cards in collections can still matter, but many are now just unpaid contracts that may or may not still be active in court. John does not need to know every law himself, but he does need to understand that some debts can chase him harder than others.

Step Three: Stabilize His Monthly Life

Before John pays old debts, he must stabilize his current life. He looks at his income and basic bills. He makes sure he can cover housing, food, utilities, transport, and health needs first. There is no point in fixing credit if he risks losing his home or his job.

He then builds a very small buffer, even if it is only a few hundred dollars, so that one surprise does not knock him back. When his present life feels stable, he is ready to start a steady credit plan.

Step Four: Talk to the Tax Authorities

John owes about twenty thousand dollars in back taxes. Ignoring this debt is not safe. He should contact the tax agency and ask about a payment plan. In many cases, the agency will work with taxpayers who file their returns and make a plan they can handle. The goal is not to pay it off all at once. The goal is to stop the debt from growing and avoid stricter actions.

By setting up a simple monthly payment he can afford, John lowers his risk and begins to rebuild trust. This step does not show on his credit reports in a direct way, but it protects his future.

Step Five: Contact the SBA or Loan Servicer

John also has a five thousand dollar SBA related loan on his reports. He needs to find out if this loan is in default and if it is still handled by the SBA or by a private collector. He can contact the servicer listed on his report and ask for a clear status.

If the loan is still active and in default, he can ask if there is a plan to bring it back into good standing or to settle it. He avoids promises he cannot keep. He does not give access to his bank account until he sees any agreements in writing. His goal is to stop this debt from growing and to remove the risk of sudden collection actions.

Step Six: Review Old Credit Card Debts

John has about twenty five thousand dollars in credit card debt that has been delinquent for four to five years. Many of these accounts are likely charged off and may now sit with collection agencies. At this age, most of these debts are doing the same type of damage day after day. They may be nearing the time when they will fall off his reports, even if they are not paid.

He has a few choices here. He can:

Stay in observe mode and let time pass while he focuses on rebuilding new positive history, if he accepts that these old accounts will drop off in a few years.

Or

Slowly settle a few key accounts that he feels ready to handle, if settlement fits within his budget and long term goals.

If he chooses settlement, he needs to move with care. He asks for clear terms in writing. He avoids any agreement that causes him more harm than good. In some cases, it may make more sense to let older debts age off rather than use limited cash on old accounts that are near their natural end on his reports. For complex questions about old debt and lawsuits, talking to a local legal aid office or attorney can help.

Step Seven: Start Real Credit Repair

Now John can apply the steps from this book. He goes through his reports and looks for actual mistakes. He looks for wrong dates, wrong balances, accounts that are not his, or duplicates. He marks each one and prepares factual dispute letters.

He sends his disputes by mail with tracking. He keeps copies of each letter. He includes only honest claims and proof he can back up. His goal is not to erase his past but to make his reports accurate. When old errors are fixed, his profile becomes cleaner, and future lenders see a clearer story.

Step Eight: Build New Positive History Slowly

Once John sets his tax plan, talks to the SBA, and sends his disputes, he can begin to rebuild. His scores are low, so he will likely start with small tools. A secured credit card is a good path if he can afford a small deposit. He puts down an amount that does not strain him and uses the card lightly.

He keeps the balance under twenty percent of the limit. He pays the card on time every month. He never misses a payment. He treats it like a training tool. Over time, this new line gives him fresh positive history.

He may also use a credit builder loan from a trusted bank or credit union. These loans save the payments in a locked account and return the money to him at the end. They create a record of on time payments without large risk.

If he rents, he can look into safe rent reporting services that send his payment history to certain reporting systems. This does not replace credit cards or loans but can give extra support if it fits his budget and landlord.

Step Nine: Protect Utilization and Payment History

As John rebuilds, two things matter the most. The first is payment history. He cannot afford any new late marks. He sets up automatic payments for his new card or loan so he never misses the due date. If he ever struggles in a month, he at least pays the minimum before the due date.

The second is utilization. Even when his limits grow, he does not treat them as free money. He works to keep his balances near ten to twenty percent of his available credit. He avoids maxing out cards. When he spends, he plans how he will pay the balance down before it becomes a burden.

Step Ten: Guard Against New Traps

Now that John is working again, he will start seeing offers. Some may be for high interest cards or store cards that do not serve him well. He stays away from cards with heavy fees and bad terms. He focuses on a small set of clear, fair accounts from known banks or credit unions.

When he needs a car, he seeks preapproval from a single lender instead of letting a dealer run his credit many times. He asks clear questions before any application and confirms if the pull is hard or soft. He guards his report like a valuable asset.

Step Eleven: Track Progress Over Time

John does not expect instant miracles. He knows his credit fell over several years. It will take time to rise. He sets a reminder to check his reports a few times a year. Each time he checks, he looks for fewer errors, fewer collections, and more clean payment history.

After a year or two of steady habits, his scores can move out of the low five hundreds. As more old accounts age off and his new lines grow older, he may see large jumps. In time, he can move back toward the six hundreds and beyond.

What This Case Study Teaches

John's story shows that even after a major crisis, serious illness, and years of late payments, there is still a path forward. The plan is not built on tricks. It is built on facts.

- He learns to face his full picture.
- He stabilizes his life.
- He talks to the tax authorities and the SBA.
- He fixes real errors.
- He builds new positive accounts.
- He protects his payment history.
- He keeps his balances low.
- He avoids new traps.
- He gives time a chance to work.

Many readers of this book will see parts of themselves in John. The numbers may be different, but the feelings are the same. Fear. Shame. Confusion. This case study shows that you are not alone and that there is a path out.

Bad credit after a crisis is not a final sentence. It is a problem that can be worked through with calm steps. With patience and steady habits, even a profile in the low five hundreds can begin to heal. John's story is proof that you can start again, no matter how far you feel you have fallen.

43

Using AI After Credit Repair: How ChatGPT Helps You Build Business Credit, Increase Income, and Stay Financially Protected in 2026

AI is not only a tool for repairing your credit. It becomes even more powerful after your credit is restored. Once your score rises and your reports are clean, you move into a new financial stage where good decisions matter even more. AI helps you stay organized, avoid financial traps, grow your income, and position yourself for long-term stability.

Credit repair is the beginning. AI helps you build the future that comes after.

1. Using AI to Build Business Credit

If you want to start a business or grow a brand, AI helps you build a business credit plan that matches your personal credit. You can ask AI to:

- create a step-by-step business credit roadmap
- explain how to use your EIN number

- outline vendor accounts and starter trade lines
- help write emails to lenders
- help compare business credit cards
- help track payment reminders

AI helps you build business credit in a calm, clear, steady way so you do not repeat old mistakes.

2. Using AI to Increase Income After Repair

When your credit rises, lenders trust you more. But income still matters. AI can help you:

- explore side income ideas
- build resumes and cover letters
- analyze job listings
- compare remote work opportunities
- build a business plan
- create marketing for your small business
- identify grants or small business programs

AI makes your professional life easier and more focused so you can grow income while keeping your credit healthy.

3. Using AI to Stay Organized With Bills and Utilization

A rising credit score can fall again if habits slip. AI helps you:

- track due dates
- plan balance paydowns
- calculate utilization

- prevent late payments
- predict score impact before making decisions
- create an automated bill calendar

This protects you from falling back into old patterns.

4. Using AI to Avoid Future Scams

Financial scams are increasing, especially in credit repair and small business programs. AI helps you:

- analyze suspicious emails
- explain contracts in simple language
- identify red flags
- check whether a company follows federal rules
- compare offers before you apply

You stay safe, even when companies push aggressive or misleading offers.

5. Using AI to Prepare for Major Purchases

After credit repair, you may want to:

- buy a car
- move into a new home
- apply for a mortgage
- refinance old debts
- qualify for business funding

AI helps you compare interest rates, create budgets, understand pre-approval steps, and plan the right timing so you do not take on more than you can handle.

6. Using AI to Maintain a Strong Credit Profile

AI helps you watch over your credit month to month:

- understanding score changes
- reading updates from bureaus
- tracking disputes
- monitoring utilization
- checking for fraud
- comparing loan offers

You remain in control, not confused or overwhelmed.

7. Using AI to Avoid Returning to Debt

AI helps you rewrite habits:

- building emergency funds
- planning debt payoff strategies
- designing spending limits
- understanding the emotional triggers behind debt
- staying accountable

This helps you avoid the traps that damaged your credit in the first place.

The Goal of This Chapter

Your credit rebuild is not the end of the journey. It is the beginning. AI gives you the clarity, structure, and calm needed to build a stable financial life long after the repair process ends.

When used with care, AI becomes the tool that helps you:

- stay organized
- stay informed
- stay protected
- stay empowered

And most importantly, it helps you grow.

44

FINAL RECAP: Bad Credit Is Not the End of Your Story

Bad credit can feel like something you drag behind you. It can make you feel judged, limited, or locked out of parts of life that should be open to you. It can feel permanent when the truth is the exact opposite. Credit is not a verdict. Credit is a moving file, shaped by data, affected by law, and open to correction and rebuilding. Your score is not your identity. It is a reflection of habits and moments, and habits can change. Moments pass. Files can be repaired. And you have more power than the system ever made you believe.

If your score collapsed because of medical debt, student loans, SBA stress, pandemic hardship, job loss, EBT struggles, tax setbacks, or uneven financial seasons, this book showed you what most people never learn: you can rebuild your entire profile with clear steps, simple structure, and the real protections federal law gives you. You are not the first person to fall. You are the one who stood up.

Throughout this book you learned how the credit system actually works in 2026. You learned how the three major bureaus operate. You learned how private companies store your information, how they verify it, and how your rights fit into the process. You learned the laws that protect you, including the Fair Credit Reporting Act, the Fair Debt Collection Practices Act, and the rules that stop collectors from crossing lines. You learned your rights to accuracy, clarity, correction, fairness, and reinvestigation.

You learned how to pull your real full credit reports, not the partial summaries from apps. You learned how to read each line. You learned how to find errors. You learned what a good score means in 2026 and why the definition changed over the past decade. You learned how to protect yourself in an era shaped by Trump-era reporting shifts, Biden-era student loan reforms, and the new scoring and verification models used in 2026. You learned what changed, what did not change, and what people often misunderstand online.

You learned the truth about medical debt and federal preemption. You learned how student loan reporting works after the pandemic freeze ended. You learned how SBA EIDL and PPP loans show up only when personal guarantees are linked. You learned why IRS balances do not appear on your credit. You learned the truth about EBT and SNAP and why they do not require a credit check. You learned how to move through the politics of credit without being manipulated by rumors or fear.

You learned what creates your score. You learned how utilization drives your numbers. You learned how late payments hit your file. You learned how to control your reporting dates so your score reflects your real habits instead of temporary balances. You learned how specialty consumer reporting agencies like LexisNexis, SageStream, Innovis, CoreLogic, and ChexSystems influence verification. You learned how freezing or unfreezing these agencies affects disputes.

You learned the truth behind disputes. You learned what to challenge and what to leave alone. You learned the difference between a 609 letter and an actual legal 611 reinvestigation. You learned why templates weaken your claims and why factual letters win. You learned how collectors must respond. You learned how to avoid re-aging traps. You learned how to handle zombie debt. You learned how to negotiate. You learned how pay for delete works when used legally and respectfully.

You learned how to rebuild with new positive history. You learned how to choose the right secured cards. You learned how builder loans work. You learned how rent reporting and utility reporting help your profile. You learned about the top companies that handle rent and utility reporting and why these tools matter. You learned the truth about authorized users. You learned how tradelines work and when they help or hurt. You learned how Buy Now Pay Later services like Klarna, Afterpay, Affirm, PayPal Pay in 4, Chime MyPay, and Empower Loans affect your credit in 2026. You learned the rules behind installment loans, revolving accounts, auto loans, leases, refinancing, and inquiries.

You learned about auto loans in a way most consumers never see. You learned the difference between leasing and financing. You learned why dealerships shotgun your credit file to multiple lenders. You learned how to avoid a stack of hard inquiries. You learned how to get a preapproval that protects your score. You learned how scoring models group auto inquiries. You learned when an auto loan can actually help your rebuild and when it can overwhelm your budget.

You learned how to protect yourself from fraud. You learned how credit freezes and fraud alerts work. You learned how identity theft interacts with disputes. You learned how to file a proper identity theft report. You learned how to use federal protections for guaranteed deletions. You learned how state laws influence collection timelines and how the statute of limitations differs from the seven year reporting rule. You learned why a debt may no longer be collectible but still appear on a report. You learned how to avoid restarting old debt.

You learned how to use the CFPB complaint system when bureaus or furnishers ignore errors. You learned how to document everything. You learned how to protect yourself from credit repair scams. You learned how to identify real companies and how to avoid companies that break the Credit Repair Organizations Act.

You learned how to build business credit in a structured way. You learned how personal credit influences business credit. You learned how to choose vendors, how to open accounts, and how to create the foundation of a business profile without falling into predatory traps.

You learned the complete ninety day reset plan. You learned the six month rebuild plan. You learned how to prepare for home ownership. You learned how to rebuild after bankruptcy or avoid bankruptcy when alternatives exist. You learned how to protect your mental and emotional energy during the process.

And you learned how to use ChatGPT with clarity and safety. You learned how AI helps you read your reports, understand your data, write letters, translate collector language, and stay organized. You learned the role AI can and cannot play. You learned how to use it as a partner, not a substitute for your rights. You learned how AI helps you build business credit, compare loan offers, plan budgets, avoid scams, increase income, and stabilize your financial life after your credit is repaired.

This book covered everything the top twenty consumer searches asked for, and everything people struggle to understand when they rebuild alone. We answered the misconceptions. We corrected the myths. We replaced confusion with law. We replaced shortcuts with structure. We replaced fear with clarity.

The story you saw in the case study mirrors the story in many homes across the country. A drop in income. A pile of debt. A sharp fall in score. A sense of defeat. And then a plan. A method. A system. A path forward.

My own story stands behind this message. I rebuilt my life and my credit during recovery. I started from the bottom. I pulled my reports. I fixed what was wrong. I built what was missing. I stayed consistent. My score rose because I rose. And so will you.

The credit world changed. The laws changed. The scoring models changed. But the core truth stays the same: you have the right to correct your file, the right to protect your future, and the right to rise beyond anything that tried to hold you back.

Bad credit is not a life sentence. It is a moment. It is a file. It is data. And data can change. Your past is not your ceiling. Your score can rise. Your stability can rise. Your confidence can rise. You have the information. You have the structure. You have the plan.

You can rebuild from anywhere.

And now you know exactly how.

Bad credit can feel like something you drag behind you. It can make you feel judged, limited, or locked out of parts of life that should be open to you. It can feel permanent when the truth is the exact opposite. Credit is not a verdict. Credit is a moving file, shaped by data, affected by law, and open to correction and rebuilding. Your score is not your identity. It is a reflection of habits and moments, and habits can change. Moments pass. Files can be repaired. And you have more power than the system ever made you believe.

If your score collapsed because of medical debt, student loans, SBA stress, pandemic hardship, job loss, EBT struggles, tax setbacks, or uneven financial seasons, this book showed you what most people never learn: you can rebuild your entire profile with clear steps, simple structure, and the real protections federal law gives you. You are not the first person to fall. You are the one who stood up.

Throughout this book you learned how the credit system actually works in

2026. You learned how the three major bureaus operate. You learned how private companies store your information, how they verify it, and how your rights fit into the process. You learned the laws that protect you, including the Fair Credit Reporting Act, the Fair Debt Collection Practices Act, and the rules that stop collectors from crossing lines. You learned your rights to accuracy, clarity, correction, fairness, and reinvestigation.

You learned how to pull your real full credit reports, not the partial summaries from apps. You learned how to read each line. You learned how to find errors. You learned what a good score means in 2026 and why the definition changed over the past decade. You learned how to protect yourself in an era shaped by Trump-era reporting shifts, Biden-era student loan reforms, and the new scoring and verification models used in 2026. You learned what changed, what did not change, and what people often misunderstand online.

You learned the truth about medical debt and federal preemption. You learned how student loan reporting works after the pandemic freeze ended. You learned how SBA EIDL and PPP loans show up only when personal guarantees are linked. You learned why IRS balances do not appear on your credit. You learned the truth about EBT and SNAP and why they do not require a credit check. You learned how to move through the politics of credit without being manipulated by rumors or fear.

You learned what creates your score. You learned how utilization drives your numbers. You learned how late payments hit your file. You learned how to control your reporting dates so your score reflects your real habits instead of temporary balances. You learned how specialty consumer reporting agencies like LexisNexis, SageStream, Innovis, CoreLogic, and ChexSystems influence verification. You learned how freezing or unfreezing these agencies affects disputes.

You learned the truth behind disputes. You learned what to challenge and what to leave alone. You learned the difference between a 609 letter and an actual legal 611 reinvestigation. You learned why templates weaken your claims and why factual letters win. You learned how collectors must respond. You learned how to avoid re-aging traps. You learned how to handle zombie debt. You learned how to negotiate. You learned how pay for delete works when used legally and respectfully.

You learned how to rebuild with new positive history. You learned how to choose the right secured cards. You learned how builder loans work. You learned how rent reporting and utility reporting help your profile. You learned about the top companies that handle rent and utility reporting and why these tools matter. You learned the truth about authorized users. You learned how tradelines work and when they help or hurt. You learned how Buy Now Pay Later services like Klarna, Afterpay, Affirm, PayPal Pay in 4, Chime MyPay, and Empower Loans affect your credit in 2026. You learned the rules behind installment loans, revolving accounts, auto loans, leases, refinancing, and inquiries.

You learned about auto loans in a way most consumers never see. You learned the difference between leasing and financing. You learned why dealerships shotgun your credit file to multiple lenders. You learned how to avoid a stack of hard inquiries. You learned how to get a preapproval that protects your score. You learned how scoring models group auto inquiries. You learned when an auto loan can actually help your rebuild and when it can overwhelm your budget.

You learned how to protect yourself from fraud. You learned how credit freezes and fraud alerts work. You learned how identity theft interacts with disputes. You learned how to file a proper identity theft report. You learned how to use federal protections for guaranteed deletions. You learned how state laws influence collection timelines and how the statute of limitations differs from the seven year reporting rule. You learned why a debt may no longer be collectible but still appear on a report. You learned how to avoid restarting old debt.

You learned how to use the CFPB complaint system when bureaus or furnishers ignore errors. You learned how to document everything. You learned how to protect yourself from credit repair scams. You learned how to identify real companies and how to avoid companies that break the Credit Repair Organizations Act.

You learned how to build business credit in a structured way. You learned how personal credit influences business credit. You learned how to choose vendors, how to open accounts, and how to create the foundation of a business profile without falling into predatory traps.

You learned the complete ninety day reset plan. You learned the six month rebuild plan. You learned how to prepare for home ownership. You learned how to rebuild after bankruptcy or avoid bankruptcy when alternatives exist. You learned how to protect your mental and emotional energy during the process.

And you learned how to use ChatGPT with clarity and safety. You learned how AI helps you read your reports, understand your data, write letters, translate collector language, and stay organized. You learned the role AI can and cannot play. You learned how to use it as a partner, not a substitute for your rights. You learned how AI helps you build business credit, compare loan offers, plan budgets, avoid scams, increase income, and stabilize your financial life after your credit is repaired.

This book covered everything the top twenty consumer searches asked for, and everything people struggle to understand when they rebuild alone. We answered the misconceptions. We corrected the myths. We replaced confusion with law. We replaced shortcuts with structure. We replaced fear with clarity.

The story you saw in the case study mirrors the story in many homes across the country. A drop in income. A pile of debt. A sharp fall in score. A sense of defeat. And then a plan. A method. A system. A path forward.

My own story stands behind this message. I rebuilt my life and my credit during recovery. I started from the bottom. I pulled my reports. I fixed what was wrong. I built what was missing. I stayed consistent. My score rose because I rose. And so will you.

The credit world changed. The laws changed. The scoring models changed. But the core truth stays the same: you have the right to correct your file, the right to protect your future, and the right to rise beyond anything that tried to hold you back.

Bad credit is not a life sentence. It is a moment. It is a file. It is data. And data can change. Your past is not your ceiling. Your score can rise. Your stability can rise. Your confidence can rise. You have the information. You have the structure. You have the plan.

You can rebuild from anywhere android now you know exactly how.

Work Cited

Works Cited and Research Method Disclaimer

This book uses only publicly available federal materials, agency documents, and verified consumer protection resources. All legal and technical explanations come from open federal sources so every reader can independently confirm the information.

Paraphrased information is clearly noted. When a law, regulation, or federal rule is simplified for readability, it is presented as a paraphrase of the original source. Direct quotations appear only when taken word for word from a federal document.

Nothing in this book is legal advice. All content is educational and based on publicly accessible federal information. Anyone facing a specific legal problem should consult an attorney.

All information reflects the most verifiable rules and public guidance available for the 2025 to 2026 reporting cycle. Credit reporting policies and federal interpretations evolve. Readers are encouraged to check the most recent guidance from official federal sources.

The purpose of this Works Cited section is to show readers exactly where the factual statements came from so all information can be verified independently.

Works Cited

Chapter 2

Consumer Financial Protection Bureau. (2020). Your Money, Your Goals: Financial empowerment toolkit.

Consumer Financial Protection Bureau. (2021). Building and maintaining your credit.

Equifax Inc. (2024). Equifax company overview.

Federal Trade Commission. (2016). A summary of your rights under the Fair Credit Reporting Act.

Federal Trade Commission. (2024). AnnualCreditReport.com is the only authorized source for your free annual credit report.

myFICO. (2024). What is in my FICO scores.

National Foundation for Credit Counseling. (2024). How am I scored.

Chapter 6

Consumer Financial Protection Bureau. (2024). Disputing errors on your credit reports. https://www.consumerfinance.gov/consumer-tools/credit-reports-and-scores/disputing-errors/

Federal Trade Commission. (2023). Fair Credit Reporting Act. https://www.ftc.gov/legal-library/browse/statutes/fair-credit-reporting-act

Federal Trade Commission. (2023). How to dispute credit report information. https://www.ftc.gov

Consumer Financial Protection Bureau. (2024). Your rights under the Fair Credit Reporting Act. https://www.consumerfinance.gov

Chapter 7

Consumer Financial Protection Bureau. (2022). Medical debt and credit reporting changes.

Federal Trade Commission. (2018). Credit freeze and fraud alert changes under the Economic Growth, Regulatory Relief, and Consumer Protection Act.

White House. (2019). Statement of Administration Policy on H.R. 5332, Protecting Your Credit Score Act. The American Presidency Project.

Public Reporting. (2025). Federal court ruling vacating the CFPB medical debt rule.

Public Reporting. (2025). CFPB interpretive rule on federal preemption and state medical debt bans.

Chapter 16

Consumer Financial Protection Bureau. (2018). A summary of your rights under the Fair Credit Reporting Act. https://files.consumerfinance.gov/f/201504_cfpb_summary_your-rights-under-fcra.pdf

Consumer Financial Protection Bureau. (2018). How to dispute credit report errors (sample letter and instructions). https://files.consumerfinance.gov/f/documents/cfpb_your-money-your-goals_dispute-credit-report_handout_2018-11.pdf

Fair Credit Reporting Act, 15 U.S.C. § 1681i.

Chapter 19

Consumer Financial Protection Bureau. (2018). A summary of your rights under the Fair Credit Reporting Act. https://files.consumerfinance.gov/f/201504_cfpb_summary_your-rights-under-fcra.pdf

Fair Credit Reporting Act, 15 U.S.C. § 1681i.

Chapter 21

Fair Credit Reporting Act, 15 U.S.C. § 1681c. Fair Credit Reporting Act, 15 U.S.C. § 1681i. Fair Debt Collection Practices Act, 15 U.S.C. § 1692g.

Consumer Financial Protection Bureau. (2018). A summary of your rights under the Fair Credit Reporting Act. https://files.consumerfinance.gov/f/201504_cfpb_summary_your-rights-under-fcra.pdf

Chapter 24

Consumer Financial Protection Bureau. (2018). A summary of your rights under the Fair Credit Reporting Act. https://files.consumerfinance.gov/f/201504_cfpb_summary_your-rights-under-fcra.pdf

Fair Credit Reporting Act, 15 U.S.C. § 1681c-2.

Federal Trade Commission. (2023). Identity Theft Report and Recovery Steps. https://www.identitytheft.gov

Chapter 34

Fair Credit Reporting Act, 15 U.S.C. § 1681g. https://www.law.cornell.edu/uscode/text/15/1681g

Fair Credit Reporting Act, 15 U.S.C. § 1681i. https://www.law.cornell.edu/uscode/text/15/1681i

www.ingramcontent.com/pod-product-compliance
Lightning Source LLC
LaVergne TN
LVHW090409210926
848480LV00002B/508
9798295444920